'While the institutional church persisted in a narrative of exclusion, LGBT+ Christians gave Christian communities the quiet, persistent grace of their presence, their gifts, and their love. Now they add grace to grace by sharing the intimacy, vulnerability, and power of their stories, narratives of God's embrace. Here we have an opportunity to listen and hear anew God's resounding Yes to these siblings who have too often been told No by human voices. In hearing, we have a fresh occasion to add our Amen to God's declarations of love.'

-J. R. Daniel Kirk, *Pastoral Director, Newbigin House of Studies*

'Brandan's new book, *Our Witness*, continues his tradition of moving the Church forward in its acceptance of LGBTQ individuals and being the inclusive institution that it is meant to be. Brandan challenges us readers to listen to voices that we may never have heard before. Their stories are extremely powerful and have the ability to shift people's paradigms. I pray that many church leaders will read its pages and be transformed. It would benefit the Church and the world.'

-Rev. David W. Key, Sr., *National Board Chair, Association of Welcoming and Affirming Baptists*

D0301158

'"Speak the truth in love", the Good Book tells us, and "The truth will set you free". For LGBT Christians, speaking the truth about our lives is important, Doing so, is powerful testimony against the lies so freely spoken about us. Much of the homophobic/transphobic pastoral practice and pseudo theology that harms our people in too many church groups, is based on those lies. Countering them contributes to building new, sound theology.

'What I particularly like about this impressive collection of LGBT testimony, is its diversity: of denomination, age, and geographic region (across the USA and UK), as well sexuality and gender identity. The unusual prominence of bisexual voices, so often overlooked in bisexual erasure, is particularly welcome.

'This book richly deserves to be read by LGBT Christians, for the healing it will help to bring - and by non-LGBT Christians, who will surely learn from it about some important truths about LGBT lives.'

-**Terry Weldon**, Deputy Chair, Quest Gay Catholics

'Our Witness is a breath-taking, essential look at faithful Christians working to be the body of Christ even as Christians marginalize and reject them. I was moved to tears even as I was filled with hope—these folks represent the best of our faith.'

-**Mike McHargue**, host of The Liturgists Podcast and author of Finding God in the Waves
'In Nomad: A spirituality for travelling light Brandan Robertson, a young man with a deep faith, engaging life experience, and mature spiritual insights, shared with the

world the story of his own journey. In editing this book -
Our Witness: the unheard stories of LGBT+ Christians
- he enables and empowers others to tell their own
profoundly moving and challenging stories in a way that
invites us all to hear and to engage with them. Attentive
listening, together with active and selfless hearing, are
essential qualities to bring to bear on dialogue between
Christians, and, indeed, within a divided world.'

-Revd. Dr. Paul Colton, *Bishop of Cork, Ireland*

'The stories of witness which Christians have told, but
which have not been heard, typify much of Christian
history. The sad but powerful words of witness in this book
are a sign of the Gospel which allows LGBT+ voices to
be heard. They offer an urgent message which needs to be
heeded by Christians in this and every generation.'

-Christopher Rowland, *Dean Ireland's Professor of the
Exegesis of Holy Scripture Emeritus, University of Oxford*

'This is a tremendous collection of deeply moving stories.
Some of them are heart-rending, some wonderfully
positive, some both. I hope before long such a book will be
neither needed nor possible.'

-Revd Professor Michael J Reiss, *UCL Institute of
Education, University College London*

Our Witness

The Unheard Stories of LGBT+ Christians

Edited by
Brandan Robertson

DARTON·LONGMAN + TODD

First published in Great Britain in 2017 by
Darton, Longman and Todd Ltd
1 Spencer Court
140 – 142 Wandsworth High Street
London SW18 4JJ

ISBN 978-0-232-53325-5

A catalogue record for this book is available from the British Library

Phototypeset by Kerrypress, St Albans, AL3 8JL
Printed and bound in Great Britain by Bell & Bain, Glasgow

CONTENTS

INTRODUCTION

Not Untold, but Unheard

Brandan Robertson

The stories of LGBT+ Christians are not *untold*, but they are often *unheard*. Throughout the history of Christianity, LGBT+ people have been playing an integral role in their communities of faith, whether or not they were able to be open about their sexuality or gender identity. We have produced good fruit and often been some of the brightest lights for the Gospel of Christ in the world. But so often, when we are brave enough to speak about our sexuality or gender identity, our light is forced under a bushel and we are cast out from the communities that we have loved and served. After we are expelled for embracing our God-given identity, we are silenced. Our voices are drowned out by the sound of dogmatic preaching about being 'unnatural', 'abominations' or 'threats to family values'. Our voices are ignored by Church leaders who sit high in their positions of power, refusing to acknowledge the legitimacy of our lives and our faith for fear that doing so would threaten their own position of privilege. Our voices are even sometimes silenced by our families whose cold obedience to Church teachings lead them to force us into programmes to change our identity or push us out of their lives until we 'repent' for being who we are.

But in the midst of all of this abuse and injustice, we keep speaking. In every city, in every denomination, in every church, there are LGBT+ Christians who refuse to be silenced. Who heed the call of Christ to proclaim the truth and shine our light without fear of persecution or rejection. Who continue to fight for our place at the table of God's grace. Or who decide to make our own tables in our own faith communities that embrace the truly radical message of God's unconditional love and acceptance of all. When all of the Church tells us to sit down and be silent, we continue to speak. We continue to embrace the love of God. We continue to follow the radically subversive way of Jesus. And as we do, we're bringing the queer masses with us.

In 2015, the Pew Research Center released a poll which showed that, while every major demographic of Christians was in decline, one of the few areas where there was a steady uptick in identification as 'Christian' was among the LGBT+ community.[1] Around the world, LGBT+ Christian organisations and churches are popping up, drawing thousands upon thousands of LGBT+ people of faith and our allies together to worship, learn, and dream about how we can be more faithful disciples of Christ. And yet, a majority of Christians around the world *don't know that this is happening*. Or worse, they *deny* that this is happening, because this evidence of the Holy Spirit's work among open and proud LGBT+ people directly contradicts their theological paradigm. But when your theology and your reality come into contradiction, often it's time to rethink your *theology*.

The Spirit of God is moving among sexual and gender minorities on every continent around the world. Openly LGBT+ people are being raised to the highest levels of leadership in churches, organisations, and denominations,

1   Pew Research Center, 'America's Changing Religious Landscape', 12 May 2015.

and while those who seek to resist the evidence of the Holy Spirit's work among these devoted followers of Jesus shout loudly from their pulpits and publishing houses, it seems to me that the voices of LGBT+ Christians are only getting louder and harder to ignore. Whether worship leaders, pastors, celebrities, bloggers, activists, or laypeople, LGBT+ Christians are boldly and bravely reclaiming our rightful place in the Body of Christ. We have a story to tell, a message to share, a Gospel to proclaim. And the Church would be wise to quiet its own voice of resistance and listen to hear what the Spirit of God might be speaking through us.

My own journey of faith and sexuality has been a rough one. I first realised that I was bisexual when I was a pre-teen. I remember sitting in the back of my church, realising that I had an uncontrollable sense of attraction to another young man a few pews in front of me, and running out of the sanctuary to the bathroom to ask God to forgive me for this 'destructive' attraction and seeking to be healed. As the years went on, my commitment to Christ grew stronger, but my sexual orientation never seemed to change. When I was finally in Bible college, studying to be a pastor, I began confessing my 'struggle' to friends on my floor during our 'accountability' meetings, and quickly found that *many* of the men studying at my school *also* struggled with 'same-sex attraction'. All of us had strong callings to ministry and had flourishing relationships with God, but lived in constant terror that this fundamental part of our identity would somehow render us damaged at best, damned at worst.

The realisation of how fearful we all were about our sexuality led me on a journey of deep biblical study and prayer. I visited churches, met with theologians, read books, and began to realise that *maybe* the Bible *wasn't* quite as clear in its condemnation of LGBT+ people as I once thought. That *maybe* the openly LGBT+ Christians that I had encountered truly *did* have a relationship with God. That *maybe* God didn't make a mistake in his creation of LGBT+ people. As I began to come to these realisations, I also began a conversion therapy programme as a last-ditch effort to see if God truly desired to heal me of being bisexual. After a year of trying to be healed of my sexuality and of wrestling with God, I finally came to a sense of peace in my heart about who I was. I felt the Spirit reassuring me that I had nothing to fear. At the same time, I knew I couldn't speak about this peace and assurance to anyone in my college or my church because it would lead to certain expulsion. So I remained in hiding.

As soon as I graduated Bible college, I moved to Washington, D.C. and decided that I needed to begin to work hard to advocate on behalf of LGBT+ people in the Church. I wasn't 'out' publicly yet, but I felt the Spirit tugging at my heart, telling me that the next step in my vocation was to do work that would be incredibly costly, but essential. I stepped into the role of national spokesperson for a new organisation that had been formed called Evangelicals for Marriage Equality, founded by two straight Evangelical men from opposite sides of the political spectrum, but who both felt convicted that Evangelical Christians should not be seeking to prevent LGBT+ people from having equal rights in our society. We launched our organisation with an op-ed in *TIME* magazine, where I wrote about my own sense of conviction about how my fellow Christians were doing great damage to the cause of Christ in our world by seeking to marginalise and prevent LGBT+ people from having equal rights under the law. Within 24 hours, leaders from the Southern Baptist Convention responded to our article with their own op-ed in *TIME*, as well as on national radio, podcasts, and various other blogs and articles. Overnight, I went from being a 'faithful Christian' in the eyes of many, to a deceived heretic – and they didn't even know that I identified as LGBT+ yet.

Over the next six months, I would be invited to participate in conversations with major Evangelical leaders on radio and in front of live audiences, and every time, I was publicly shamed for my position and told that I was leading many into destruction. This experience of rejection culminated in February of 2015, when I turned in the manuscript of my first book, *Nomad*, to my Christian publisher and was abruptly told that – unless I signed a statement condemning same-sex relationships as contrary to God's created plan – then they could not publish my book. When I saw this email, I knew that I could no longer hide the truth of what I believed and where I stood in regard to my own sexuality. I wrote back to my publisher and let them know that I wouldn't sign their statement, and soon after was told that my book contract had been cancelled. When news of this story reached a reporter at *TIME*, she told me that she wanted to write a story about this loss, but that she wanted to tell the *full* story, including the truth about my sexuality. At this point, I knew it was time. I knew that if I remained closeted and hiding in fear, I would be doing more harm than good for myself and for the LGBT+ people who were being affected by the public work I was engaged in. I agreed to let the reporter write a story, under the condition that I would be given a few weeks to come out to my friends and family. She agreed, and we moved forward with the story.

Just a few days after talking with the reporter, I was sitting in a room playing a game with some friends and my phone began to vibrate uncontrollably. Message after message began to pour in by the dozens. I had no clue what was going on. I opened my text-messaging app and saw that the first message was from the reporter at *TIME* – 'I'm so sorry! My editors published the piece early by mistake!' her message read. I felt my heart skip a beat, as I scrolled over to Facebook to find myself tagged in a headline that said 'Young Evangelical Leader Loses Book Deal After Coming Out'.[2] The only problem with the headline was that I *hadn't* come out to most of my friends or family yet, and the flurry of messages I received were from people in my life responding, with both affirmation and strong condemnation, to the revelation of my true sexual identity. The next few days are now a blur to me, but they were filled with some of the warmest embraces and coldest condemnations from various mentors and friends in my life. My family reacted surprisingly well, which was a relief. But some of my closest mentors filled my inbox with messages like:

> I wonder [if] you tell the people how dishonest, cunning and manipulative you are. I wonder whether you tell them about your addictions and compulsions. I wonder whether you tell them about how actively you cultivate a sin life while being so inactive towards righteousness and how damningly lazy you are? Do you tell them how disinterested you are in the Word? So where exactly do the bridges you allegedly build lead? Certainly you are a leader, Brandan. It is safe to say that in the current trajectory of your life you will usher many into a hellish existence.

2   See the article here: *TIME*, 'Young Evangelical Leader Loses Book Deal After Coming Out' (21 February 2015), http://time.com/3716350/brandan-roberston-destiny-image/.

And when you need the blood of Christ to wash away your sins, where will you turn, now that you have renounced His redeeming and transforming work so thoroughly? I know you like to be coddled. True words feel so harsh to you. (This, of course, keeps the door to your personal prison locked.) Nevertheless, only one word makes sense to speak: Repent.[3]

I had experienced rejection for my support of marriage equality before, but now that I was publicly identified as LGBT+, the words of condemnation I received were harsher and more cutting than ever. For the first time, I really experienced the harm and deep wounding that so many of my LGBT+ friends had told me about. I knew this would someday be a reality that I faced, but I had never really counted the cost. Now, I was being personally attacked by those who once loved me; I was told that my future in pastoral ministry within my Evangelical context would never be a reality; and I became a scapegoat for so many non-affirming Christians to throw all sorts of accusations upon.

When all of this was happening, I entered into a period of severe sorrow. But it wasn't sorrow for myself or my future – I believed that I would make it through this and was relentlessly committed to pursuing my calling regardless of what my opponents said. My grief instead was for the Church. A community of people who have committed their lives to follow the life and teachings of Jesus, who so quickly had turned to cast stones at me and so many other LGBT+ people simply because they disagreed with

---

3   This is a quote from an actual email I received from an actual former mentor of mine. Some details of the quote have been omitted or changed for privacy reasons.

us over the interpretation of six verses in the Bible. Until I experienced the full force of rejection and condemnation of many in the Church, I never truly understood just how *unchristlike* the Church's posture towards LGBT+ people really was. On dozens of important theological and social issues, Christians have agreed to remain in unity in the midst of their disagreements. But on this one issue, one that affects so many people at the most intimate levels of their Being, the Church has chosen a posture of full-on attack and rejection, and in doing so, has isolated and harmed so many beautiful, talented, faithful followers of Christ.

My sorrow over the Church's response to LGBT+ people has continued to this day, but it has now largely been overshadowed by a profound, subversive hope. Over the past five years, I have met *thousands* of LGBT+ Christians around the world, and have witnessed the work of the Holy Spirit moving through them in the most profound ways. I have been blown away by how many major, global Christian leaders have reached out to tell me that they too have felt the Spirit of God nudging them to step forward and embrace LGBT+ people as faithful members of Christ's Church. I have watched as societies around the world have stepped closer and closer to affirming and embracing LGBT+ people as equal and essential parts of their communities. And I have seen *true revival* breaking forth in the midst of LGBT+ Christian communities. So, while I am continually grieved as I watch my brave LGBT+ siblings step out of the darkness and into the light of who God made them to be and be subsequently abused by Christians, I am also profoundly confident that this movement that we are a part of is a movement of the Holy Spirit of God, and that nothing and no one will be able to stop this wild river of inclusion.

The more that straight, non-affirming Christians witness the work of God in and through the lives and stories of LGBT+ people, the more I see hearts of stone soften, and the doors of churches open just a little wider to welcome LGBT+ people into our rightful place at the table of Grace.

And *that* is the inspiration and vision behind this book. Because I believe that God is doing a new thing through LGBT+ people, and I also believe that the only way for anyone to truly understand this movement of God is to hear the authentic, raw stories of LGBT+ Christians. Since the very beginning of our faith, Christians have been a people of *story* and of *testimony*. We have always known that when people hear our stories and experience life through our eyes, hearts and minds will change. And these brave siblings of mine have poured out their souls onto these pages, giving you a glimpse into their authentic struggles, pains, and triumphs. It is truly a *sacred privilege* to be invited into these lives together, and I hope that as you read these words, you feel humbled by the invitation that has been extended.

My hope for this book is twofold: first, that LGBT+ Christians and our allies will be able to hear the powerful witness contained in these stories and find strength, encouragement, and hope to continue to press on in our fight for inclusion. For my LGBT+ Christian siblings, I want you to know that you're not alone and that there *is* great reason to hope. For our allies, I hope that these stories add fuel to your fire, and that you will be moved to find ways to uplift the unheard voices of LGBT+ Christians in your communities.

Second, I challenge non-affirming Christians to read these stories in their entirety, without looking for points of disagreement or debate, but instead hearing the truth of the experiences of these LGBT+ Christians. As you read, I challenge you to be in prayer, opening yourself to whatever the Spirit of God might be saying to you through each life that is poured out in these pages. My goal isn't to convince you to change your mind necessarily, but for you to develop empathy and consider the great harm that has been done in the name of Jesus by those who hold your theological commitments. And after reading these stories, I hope that you will reach out to an LGBT+ person in your community and ask them to share with you their story as well, and that you might posture yourself in humility and repentance for the harm that has been done in the name of Christ by non-affirming Christians.

More than anything, my hope is that these words, these stories, these *lives* will bear witness to the power of the love of God and the truly good news of the Gospel. I pray that, as our collective light shines forth, many would see the good work that God is doing in and through us, and be moved to worship our expansive, diverse, and inclusive Creator. May it be.

SECTION 1: REJECTION

One of the most basic Christian tests for determining the truth of a doctrine or practice is based on the teaching of Jesus in the Gospel of Matthew, where he proclaims that one way his disciples can determine between true prophets and false prophets is 'by their fruits'.[1] This language of 'fruits' appears numerous times throughout the New Testament[2] and refers to the familiar first-century agricultural imagery, which suggests that some crops yield 'good fruits', or a harvest that is luscious, edible, and profitable, compared to those crops that yield 'bad fruits', or a harvest that is diseased and scarce. Throughout the New Testament, we are continually reminded that faithful followers of Jesus will bear 'good fruits', or what the Apostle Paul calls 'fruits of the spirit'.[3] If one takes this call to discernment and examination of Christian teaching seriously, it naturally leads one to ask the question: what is the result of a teaching on the lives of those who receive it? If a teaching produces life and love, one could make the case that it bears good fruits, and therefore is a faithful and true teaching. Jesus' own life serves as our example of what good fruit looks like: standing up for the oppressed,

1   Matthew 7:16.
2   Matthew 3:8–10; 7:16–20; 12:33; 21:43; Luke 6:43; John 15:5; Romans 7:4; Galatians 5:22.
3   Galatians 5:22.

welcoming the marginalised, and healing those who have been harmed by religious and political powers. But what if a teaching produces death, mental harm, and fear? It seems that, following the logical pattern set forth in the Scriptures, we should condemn this teaching because of its 'bad fruit' and it should be 'cut down and thrown into the fire'[4] or hastily disregarded as 'false'.

Yet, when it comes to the teachings of the Church about non-inclusion, this biblical standard has been largely disregarded. Over the past decade, dozens of peer-reviewed studies have demonstrated a clear link from non-inclusive religious teachings and practices to higher rates of depression and suicide in sexual and gender minorities. In 2012, the European Symposium on Suicide and Suicidal Behaviour released a groundbreaking survey which suggested that suicide rates among LGBT+ youth were significantly higher if the youth grew up in a religious context.[5] Similarly, dozens of studies carried out between 2001 and 2015 have found links between religious affiliation and higher rates of depression and suicidality among LGBT+ adults.[6] A study published in 2014 by Jeremy Gibbs concluded:

4　Matthew 7:19.
5　Jewish Press Staff, 'Study: Highest Suicide Rates Among Religious Homosexuals', *Jewish Press* (2012), www.jewishpress.com/news/breaking-news/study-highest-rate-of-suicide-among-religious-homosexuals/2012/09/05/.
6　The following is a sampling of the multiple surveys and studies that I have examined: R.R. Ganzevoort, M. Van der Laan and E. Olsman, 'Growing up gay and religious. Conflict, dialogue, and religious identity strategies', *Mental Health, Religion, and Culture* 14 (2011), 209–222; J.J. Gibbs, 'Religious conflict, sexual identity, and suicidal behaviors among LGBT young adults', *Archives of Suicide Research* 19 (2015), 472–88; J.T. Goldbach, E.F. Tanner-Smith, M. Bagwell and S. Dunlap, 'Minority stress and substance use in sexual minority adolescents: a meta-analysis', *Prevention Science* 15 (2014), 350–63; A.H. Grossman and A.R. D'Augelli, 'Transgender youth and life-threatening behaviors', *Suicide and Life-Threatening Behavior* 37 (2007), 527–37; V. Figueroa and F. Tasker, '"I always have the idea of sin in my mind. …": Family of origin, religion, and Chilean young gay men', *Journal of GLBT Family Studies* 10 (2013), 269–97.

[Sexual minority youth (SMY)] who mature in religious contexts, which facilitate identity conflict, are at higher odds for suicidal thoughts and suicide attempt compared to other SMY.[7]

Every year, new studies come out which suggest that non-inclusive religious teachings result in higher rates of depression and suicidal ideation among LGBT+ youth and adults alike. These facts must be heeded by those in Christian leadership and lead to deep reflection on how their teaching and practices are complicit in these concerning trends.

While many conservative religious commentators have strongly pushed back against any suggestion that their theology has any actual effect on LGBT+ mental health and suicide rates, and in fact, will often use these statistics to suggest that it is not their teachings but rather the 'gay lifestyle' that contributes to the mental distress of LGBT+ people,[8] these numbers and the experiences of LGBT+ people simply cannot be denied or ignored. Religious teachings that perpetuate the idea that sexual and gender minorities are somehow disordered, flawed, or sinful because of this piece of their identity have direct effects on the mental health of these individuals. Likewise, when straight congregants digest these teachings and are left to implement them practically in their own lives as they relate to LGBT+ people, it often translates to harsh rejection and condemnation. If the LGBT+ person is a youth, they

7   Jeremy Goldbach, *Growing Up Queer and Religious: A Quantitative Study Analyzing the Relationship between Religious Identity Conflict and Suicide in Sexual Minority Youth* (University of Southern California, 2013), N.p.: 141st APHA Annual Meeting and Exposition.

8   For examples, see Dr Michael Brown's interview where he suggests that LGBT+ rights activists use suicide victims as pawns to perpetuate the gay agenda: www.rightwingwatch.org/post/michael-brown-gays-use-youth-suicide-victims-as-pawns/.

may be forced into reparative therapy programmes, a pseudo-psychological practice that has been condemned by every reputable[9] psychological association in the US as dangerous to the health and wellbeing of LGBT+ people.[10] If a youth chooses to embrace their sexuality or gender identity, they are likely to be kicked out of their homes, driving up the rates of LGBT+ youth homelessness, which currently represents between 20 and 40 per cent of all homeless youth.[11]

As one examines the evidence closely, the fruit of non-inclusive religious teaching and practice is undeniably clear – it breeds death, rejection, and severe psychological damage on sexual and gender minorities. It follows that these teachings should be 'cast into the fire'[12] and religious theologians and practitioners of all stripes should be led back to their sacred texts and traditions to reassess the messages they are preaching, seeking to listen closely to the voice of the Spirit for a message that is truly good news and brings life to all people.

The following stories focus on the harm of rejection and the incredible damage done by non-affirming theology and practice. Each of these stories goes into tremendous detail describing just how destructive non-inclusion can be. The question that I invite you to consider as you read

9   By 'reputable', I am referring to psychological associations that engage in peer-reviewed studies and have been validated by the US Government as reliable sources of information, as opposed to the many smaller religiously rooted psychological associations that are seen by the mainstream psychological community as engaging in a form of pseudo-psychology.

10   Human Rights Campaign, 'Policy and Position Statements on Conversion Therapy', Human Rights Campaign (2012), www.hrc.org/resources/policy-and-position-statements-on-conversion-therapy.

11   Ray Nicholas, *Lesbian, Gay, Bisexual, and Transgender Youth: An Epidemic of Homelessness* (National Gay and Lesbian Task Force Policy Institute, 2006), http://www.thetaskforce.org/static_html/downloads/reports/reports/HomelessYouth_ExecutiveSummary.pdf

12   Matthew 7:19.

through each one of these accounts is this: could a true teaching of Christ *really* produce such harm? If the truth is supposed to produce *good fruit* and set people free, why then are an overwhelming majority of LGBT+ people so tremendously harmed by the Church's teachings and practices in relation to their sexual orientation or gender identity? When our teaching and practice produces such pain and damage, perhaps it is time that we acknowledge they do not find their origin in God, and should be repented of and discarded for the good of our LGBT+ siblings in Christ.

Gatekeeper

Jonathan Brower

Jonathan Brower is a Canadian theatre artist and writer who uses art as a vehicle for empathy, education and activism. He holds a BFA in Drama and a BA in Communications Studies from the University of Calgary. Jonathan is currently pursuing a Masters in Social Justice & Equity at Brock University in Ontario. His quarter-century journey to self-acceptance led him to found a queer theatre company and create 'oblivion', a touring performance that illuminates the complexity of trying to reconcile faith and sexuality. Follow Jonathan @RegardingDis

Gatekeeper,

You cannot expect your people to practise what you preach, when they do not know what you practise.

You ask us to put ourselves at risk to be present so those who would hurt us and judge us and misunderstand don't have to feel uncomfortable.

We sit in fear so you can pretend to shepherd all your sheep equally. You are asking us to be brave until you can be. Until you are no longer ruled by fear.

You allow us to be devalued because you fear the rejection of the powerful.

Our Witness

You use our absence against us as if asking for full affirmation is too much too soon.

You use our presence against us as if we are proof that the current state of things is enough and does not pain us incredibly.

When we stay, we hope for change in the midst of a dangerous place. We are not your credit for things well done. We are not your trophies or your liquid gold.

We endure with you only through the Spirit, which moves us to love you and your people more than you can love us.

We are here to help you see. But we are not invincible.

By the time you reach your perfect way, your perfect moment, your perfect method; when all seems ready, you will have lost us.

What's it to you to lose one queer sheep for the sake of thousands? Christ would have stayed with the 99. That's what He said right?

How long will you use our names in vain for the sake of those who would leave your Church because they can't stand our equality?

We are asking for an equal place at His table. Christ has already granted us that. Why will you not follow His lead?

We will not be the excuse for a split; we will not be their excuse to leave.

Our inclusion will not exclude – it will only reveal those who would turn us away from God's love to uphold their own selfish convictions.

Section 1: Rejection

We are not unholy. By accepting us, you do not accept immorality. You have the witness and the theology to prove this.

We will be the revelation that illuminates those who desire to truly follow Christ, and those who cannot accept to love their neighbour as themselves.

I know you probably believe that you have nothing against us; that you and your Church love us.

But we know good fruit when we see it.

Gatekeeper, won't you open your eyes?

Love does no harm.

The Crimson River

Katy-Anne Binstead

Katy-Anne Binstead is a single mother with four children, a happy liberal, and committed Episcopalian. She grew up in Australia but now has US citizenship. She is currently studying a Master of Arts in English and creative writing at Southern New Hampshire University and holds a Bachelor of Arts (Honours) from CQUniversity, Australia.

The blade plunged into me as I drew it across my skin causing an ugly red line of blood. I licked off the blood and continued with the practice, making sure to punish myself severely. I needed to punish myself because my very existence was an abomination to God. I was a young woman who was equally attracted to both men and women, and my religion taught that that was sin against a holy God. So, I would cut myself as atonement for my sin, forgetting that Jesus has already atoned for my sins (of which I had plenty but being bisexual wasn't one of them).

The deed done, I hoped that God would forgive me for a while longer of being attracted to women as well as men, for looking at lesbian porn as well as regular porn, and for dating a hot woman. I had carefully hidden this part of my life from my fundamentalist church because I would have been disciplined by the Church had they found out and probably even thrown out of the Church. At the time, church was the only life that I knew. They were family to me. I had no other friends, just those at church – as well as the young woman I was in a relationship with.

When it became obvious that I was still acting out on my sexuality, I sunk the blades in deeper, trying to kill myself, hoping that the ultimate act of death would atone for being such an abomination. At least I wouldn't be an abomination if I were dead. I figured that God would rather have me dead than to continue to live in such gross sin.

After my suicide mission failed – because I didn't have the heart to end it all, because part of me wanted to live even as an abomination – I decided to 'repent' of my 'sin'. After an appropriate period of private repentance, I tearfully admitted to my best friend at the time and missionary that I had once been a lesbian. It was a very painful thing for me to admit and I wasn't sure she would forgive me even though God supposedly had. I became a poster child for the ex-gay movement in my small circle of churches. I claimed to have been an ex-lesbian because that is how I understood myself at the time, because I hadn't even heard of bisexual. But my whole life I had heard that being gay or lesbian, or 'homosexual' or 'queer' as it was called in our house, was the worst sin you could commit against God.

This meant that I wasn't just a sinner. I was the worst sinner that ever lived because I had been in relationships with women. I deserved to be cast out of my family and the Church, to be put to death, and then to burn in hell forever, because nobody who was LGBT was apparently a Christian. So, despite the fact that I had 'been saved' over and over again, it obviously didn't stick because I had been a lesbian. I was a disgusting piece of trash who wasn't worthy of God's love.

Come to find out you can't pray the gay away. When I realised that, I grudgingly admitted that I was bisexual. I thought that it was one thing to be bisexual, but it was still a sin to be in relationships with women. In other words, I was still broken and still disgusting but as long as I didn't act on it I could maybe be at the bottom of God's totem pole rather than not being on it at all. I was upset with God because I couldn't figure out why I had to be bisexual and all the straight people had it easy. I didn't know why I had been given such a burden and I wished I could figure out what made me bisexual.

Then came the lowest point of my entire life. My husband, who I had married as part of my repentance, had cheated on me with multiple women and my children were taken away by the state for a mistake that he made. When it was so dark and I couldn't see through the dark I had to cling to the light of the world which is Jesus. As I clung to Jesus, I began to be closer to him. As the darkness began to dissipate, I began to realise that God had created me to be bisexual – and living that out would mean that God was delighted because God had handcrafted me that way. God made me bisexual so it pleased God when I lived out my sexuality in full integrity.

I could finally be at peace with being bisexual, knowing that God created me that way and the Bible says that God looked at humankind and said that our creation was 'very good'. God had created me. God had created my sexuality as part of me. God had made me bisexual because God thought that it was very good to do so. I needed to accept myself the way that God had crafted me. God thought that I was very good.

At the utmost lowest part of my life I found peace with being bisexual. I was twenty-eight years old. I had just left fundamentalism and was attending an Episcopal

Church which has been very healing for me. I was drawn to liturgical worship at a time when my soul was starved and I needed the Eucharist. Consuming Jesus in the Eucharist made me realise that God loved me and that I was a special creation of God's. That the verse about being fearfully and wonderfully made isn't just a verse for pro-lifers to use in their fight against abortion but that it was true for me. I was fearfully and wonderfully made as a special creation. It's been healing to be in a Church where my sexuality is affirmed. Some people don't have that luxury.

I no longer have to hide myself from God and from the Church, because who I am is a delight to the one who made me. I'm in a denomination that celebrates who I am, which is a huge blessing. I now have friends who also accept me as a bisexual woman who is their sister in Christ. I can be thankful that God created me this way and I'm assured of God's love for me. I'm not an abomination. I'm a beautiful woman created in God's image to worship God.

I still have scars from the crimson river. I have covered some of them up with a tattoo that says 'grace' because God's grace kept me alive when I tried to end it all. I have a large crucifix tattooed to my left shoulder to have Jesus close to my heart and to remember that God made me who God wanted me to be, and that I need to live out that reality in my life, because that is how to please God.

A Wild Adventure

Bernárd Lynch

Bernárd Lynch studied at the African Missions College, 26 miles from Belfast. He worked with the Bemba people for two years in North Central Zambia. He has an interdisciplinary doctorate in counselling psychology and theology from Fordham University and New York Theological Seminary. For 15 successive years he was theological consultant to the Board of Directors of Dignity New York and founded their AIDS/HIV ministry in 1982. For more than ten years, Bernárd was a member of the Mayor of New York's voluntary task force on HIV/AIDS, and was the only Roman Catholic priest to testify before the city council for the successful passage of civil rights legislation for the LGBT community in 1986. He has been profiled three times on Channel 4 (UK). In February 1993 his book, A Priest on Trial, *was published by Bloomsbury, London, and Circle Books published his book* If It Wasn't Love *in 2011. He continues his work for justice.*

As a young boy on Europe's most western seaboard, the Atlantic coast of Ireland, I was told that playing 'footsie' with the girl next door was wrong and shameful. 'Footsie', to my unknowing reader, is a game which children play usually in spring or summertime. It consists simply of taking off one's shoes and socks and sitting facing each other. Each player tries to push the other contestant with his or her bare feet. The one who succeeds in pushing hardest usually wins. It is a simple and childish game and one may rightfully assume quite innocent, but this innocence was poisoned at the well of its own birth. I was not really sure why this was so. The invoking of telling the priest if we did not put our shoes back on immediately lodged in my young mind as there being something very wrong with flesh touching flesh.

The message landed indelibly on my soul. Sensual pleasure was wrong and against the priest and therefore God. This birth pang of Irish Jansenism and toxic shame has been the bane of my life. Sensual and sexual pleasure is almost a guarantee of a hot and humid eternity. Despite 25 years of psychotherapy and sexual experience, I still find it very difficult to connect my soul to my body in the act of making love to my lover and life partner of over 20 years.

It is never too late to have a happy childhood. Yet, I believe the brown paper bag we inherit from our childhood profoundly affects our living and loving all of our lives. While I am still Catholic and a priest, I don't know if the bag in which these two gifts were delivered has at times outweighed the beauty of the gift of faith. This gift of faith I do cherish more than any other. The paradox being that it has and does profoundly affect in a negative sense the integration of my gay sexuality. I do know that I am not alone in this. Many straight Catholic people I have met and ministered to, together with others of different religions and none, have likewise been warped by religious enculturation and indoctrination.

The Word made flesh in the lives and loves of so many Christians has *de facto* been the Word made muck. This cannot be right, from either a human or a religious point of view. What is it one may well ask about our enfleshed desires that seems to frighten off so-called 'spiritual' people? Or what is it about the Spirit or religious life that immediately seems to be antithetical to a life of human fleshly love? One would think that God having become human flesh in Christ is enough validation for us to be free to engage and enjoy relationships without all this policing of sexual desire, for which the Catholic Church in particular and other religious bodies in general are so famous.

Sex can and does go wrong. So does every human activity, even that of the most noble and altruistic kind. But why does sex receive such binding with briars throughout Christian history? This is more than just a means of controlling people. It is certainly that. If one controls how a social group relate and breed, then that most definitely will define everything from people's economic to private lives. As in my own story, as soon as the dialectics of power are remotely threatened by the suggestion that an alternative way of loving is possible, then the entire might of institutional power comes cascading down.

From the dawning of my own consciousness as a gay man, I have tried within the limitations of my humanity to seek the professional help I needed to integrate my God-given sexuality with the rest of my humanity. As part of the process of engaging in that endeavour, I have also worked assiduously for LGBT freedom. This struggle within me and outside of me has necessarily been at a certain cost. I realised very early that anyone who goes after freedom and justice – either for oneself or others – is going to face opposition. Identifying with the oppressed and powerless inevitably means being oppressed along the road to freedom. This was never clearer to me than in the midst of the AIDS pandemic in New York City in the 1980s. As hundreds of our friends and associates died around us, we fell out of our closets and took to the streets to seek protection in jobs and housing for our most vulnerable sisters and brothers. It was in the Dickensian sense 'the best of times and the worst of times'. There was very little time to think – what was needed was action. People were sick and dying and being ignored by Church and state authorities. Worse still, our gay brothers were being blamed for their illness. The first statement from the Vatican by a then Monsignor, now Archbishop Foley was, 'AIDS is the natural result of unnatural acts.'

I went to City Hall in New York in 1986 to testify before the city council for the passage of 'Intro. 2', a civil rights bill that would guarantee lesbians and gays protection against discrimination in jobs and housing. The proposed legislation had been defeated in council for ten years running. Its chief opponent was the Archdiocese of New York. The Archdiocese used all of its political muscle to force Catholic politicians to defeat the bill. John Cardinal O'Connor led the opposition with his famous line of attack, 'God's law cannot be changed.' How the Cardinal succeeded in mangling God's law into discrimination against a struggling and now dying minority I shall never know. On hearing of the Church's opposition, and being steeped in ministry to gay people suffering and dying from HIV/AIDS, I joined the struggle for justice and testified for the bill. The bill passed. The battle had begun.

In 1984, my closest priest friend and former professor and confessor died of complications related to HIV/AIDS. He had been working at the school, Mount Saint Michael Academy in the Bronx, where I was campus minister. On his death, his brother and fellow priest started a witch-hunt at the school to have me ousted from my position. He blamed me for his beloved brother's death. He arrived at the Academy several times with placards denouncing me publicly as an 'avowed homosexual' and a 'danger to the students'.

I was theological consultant to Dignity New York, an organisation for the pastoral and social support of lesbian and gay Catholics and their friends. As for all gay organisations in the city at that time, the AIDS pandemic was having a devastating effect on our membership. As a priest ministering to the community, I was necessarily deeply committed to care for those who were sick and dying. Consequently, I started the first pastoral care service for people with AIDS in the city in 1982. I soon found myself drafted onto New York Mayor Edward Koch's task force on HIV/AIDS. While this particular work was demanding, enervating, and challenging, it did not interfere with my duties as campus minister to Mount Saint Michael Academy. Although my religious superiors were aware of my work with Dignity, they had no difficulty with it. In fact, many of my colleagues both admired and supported me. I was out as a gay man to all of my friends, but not in the school to my pupils or most of the faculty.

When my sexual orientation came into the public forum through the witch-hunt, there was initially no outcry. The principal of the school remained silent, but not for long. Three teachers on the faculty joined in the witch-hunt and formed a group called SAFE (Students Against Faggots in Education). The group's leaders went to the principal demanding my resignation. I was summoned to the principal's office and told that I would have to go. I protested my complete innocence and told the school authorities that in no way would I be scapegoated in this fashion. I was also pertinently aware that the principal was gay and had been seen by many of my friends in Dignity in gay bars in the city. Eventually 'for the good of the school'

I agreed to resign and was given a full year's salary with excellent references. The principal died of AIDS-related illness two years later.

I took advantage of my forced resignation to throw myself headlong into my pastoral ministry with those in our community suffering and dying from HIV/AIDS. The Archdiocese of New York was not at all happy and would not renew my faculties (licence) to minister as a priest. I tried several other bishops, but everywhere I went I was blackballed. Eventually, my religious superiors were forced by Cardinal O'Connor to order me to Rome. My stay there, although orchestrated by the Congregation for the Doctrine of the Faith (formerly the Inquisition) under the control of Cardinal Ratzinger (later Pope Benedict XVI), was pleasant enough. I stayed in my Religious Order's Society of African Missions headquarters and studied French and Marian spirituality at the Angelicum and Gregorian universities. I was ordered by Cardinal Ratzinger to be faithful to Church teachings. Subsequently I had to sign a document to that effect. I had no difficulty in so doing, as I made clear to my own superiors. Pursuing justice for the oppressed and caring for the sick and dying was to my mind the most sacred duty the Church had in light of the Gospel of Jesus Christ.

In Rome I made contact with the local HIV/AIDS support groups for gay men. I was shocked but not surprised to learn that there was no support whatsoever from any of the thousands of Church bodies in Rome. I invited them to a Mass and social at my Religious Society's headquarters. They expressed their hurt and anger at the Church and deep-felt gratitude for our hospitality. As I learned, there was no gay scene in the Eternal City. Everything was underground and buried in shame and secrecy. There was lots of sex available, but few bars or centres in which people could meet and form loving and lasting relationships. Undoubtedly, this was a direct result and consequence of the Catholic Church's condemnation and unmitigated oppression of gay people. 'Don't humanise your sexuality' was and very often still is the unspoken but unquestionable message of the Church to sexual minorities. The very same Church that condemns gay men for sexual promiscuity promotes it in every single utterance from its magisterium.

While in Rome, the Cardinal Archbishop in New York was making sure that I would not return. Together with the help of the Federal Bureau of Investigation (FBI) and SAFE at my former school, the witch-hunt took on a new momentum. The FBI with the New York City vice squad started an investigation of 'certain goings-on' that had been reported to them by 'concerned church authorities' and some teachers. At first, my name did not surface as one to be investigated. I had already been out of the school for four years. Eventually when my name was mentioned, a seventeen-year-old student claimed – under pressure and questionable ethical tactics by the investigating agent – that I had molested him as a fourteen-year-old. I was on retreat in Dublin preparing for my return to HIV/AIDS ministry in New York when I received the word from my Provincial Superior headquarters in Ireland. The Provincial told me that the FBI was looking for me. I had absolutely no idea why. I was not left in the dark for long. After some excellent legal advice, paid for by my religious community, I returned to New York in a hail of media publicity to face the charges brought against me.

At the time I was given very little hope of justice. After all I was up against two of the most formidable and powerful institutions in the world: the Catholic Church and the FBI. For almost an entire calendar year, together with my defence team and loyal friends, I went back and forth to the Bronx Supreme Court to try to clear my name of these outrageous and calumnious charges. Eventually, on 21 April 1989, the plaintiff John Schaefer refused to testify. Having admitted that he had been forced against his will to bring the charges by Special Agent McDonald, he refused to go further with the case. Schaefer was nineteen years of age at the time. The judge, the Honourable Burton Roberts, not only dismissed the charges, but also declared me fiercely innocent in the entire case.

It was a pyrrhic victory. The effects of this soul murder by the Church I served and devoted my life to in New York will pursue me to the grave. After the trial, I could no longer work for the Church there. I remained in priestly ministry and continued my pastoral care for people who were HIV positive. Eventually I felt I had to get out of the city and migrate to London. At least, I thought to myself, if I get away from all the politics and publicity for a while, maybe I could return and start anew? I was wrong. Time, like God, is on the side of love and the arc of justice does bend towards freedom. While as a priest I am still part of the institutional Church, I do believe all institutional religion is about the denial of God. In transcending institutional religion, to live out my ministry, I have come closer to that 'knowledge that surpasses knowledge'. When I arrived in London in the spring of 1992 I never thought that here God's love in Christ would become truly incarnational. All of my life I had dreamt of some day meeting another man with whom I could live a life of love. In London I found my future husband. As Catholics, our human communion has become for us Holy Communion. This coming year, we are getting married on the wild Atlantic coast of Ireland. We have arrived from where we started and know it for the first time. Its name and nature is Love.

Intentionally Woven

Isaac Archuleta

Isaac Archuleta MA LPC is a professional counsellor and former seminary professor who founded iAmClinic, a Denver-based counselling practice devoted to the LGBTQ community and their religious parents. Isaac also serves as the Interim Executive Director of the Gay Christian Network. Being an ethnic and sexual minority, professional clinician, and a Christian, Isaac considers it his life's work to address the socio-religious mechanisms that mitigate psychological and spiritual development. Isaac is often heard on various podcasts and can be seen throughout the US speaking at religious and counselling psychology conferences. Isaac hosts regional training for clergy and psychotherapists, contributes to The Huffington Post, and has been featured on National Public Radio (NPR). For more information, visit IsaacArchuleta.com or iAmClinic.org.

My father spent every second of his leisure hours building a clubhouse for me the summer I turned eleven. I would stand watching him labour away from inside the house, wondering why he didn't want my company. I wanted nothing more than to matter to my father. I wanted him to see me as a spectacular version of a boy, so much so that I would captivate his heart, like any good son. But each nail he hammered was another nail in the coffin. From behind the windowpane, I could hear the echoes of the hammer reverberating through the house. I took his silence as panging rejection. To him, I didn't matter, or so I thought.

Years later, he was preaching in the church he had started in the basement of our small home. The tone of this particular sermon left panic booming within my chest – sinners would go to hell, most precisely the homosexuals. They, he told us, would burn because they *made* God angry. When my father delivered this sermon, I was a senior in high school. I had already lost my virginity to my high school sweetheart, Victoria. I loved Victoria very much and found our sexual rendezvous to be very thrilling and deeply satisfying, but I was also attracted to the same gender. I hid my attractions for the same gender, not because I was embarrassed, but because outing myself, especially to my parents, meant that I was a failed boy – a damaged son.

After trying to please God and my parents by fulfilling the Christian list of moral standards, my body betrayed me. I couldn't control the responses of my heart and sexuality. It wasn't as though I had *done* something wrong. It was that I *was* something wrong, damaged from the deepest core of my being. Even my innocent desires to love and be loved were disordered.

I drove home from church that afternoon with tears flowing down my cheeks and dripping from my chin. Although I had prayed every day since the age of nine, asking God to take away my femininity and attractions for other boys my age, I was still broken. God didn't want to or couldn't help me. I was told that if I had shown God my seriousness and determination that he could take any discomfort from my life or any distortion from my emotional body. So, I fasted two meals every day for my entire senior year of high school. When my attractions persisted, I gave up on God.

Surely I had done everything I could to make God happy with me. I interpreted God's despondence as rejection. I was sixteen years old with a pit in my stomach that left me feeling utterly valueless. As a means to soothe the utterly debilitating sense of failure and hopelessness, I began drinking. During the last semester of my high school career, I reached blackout drunk three times a week. My parents never knew.

Psychology quickly grabbed my attention in college and I soaked in its lessons. I was desperately trying to fix myself. And when the undergraduate courses left me more hungry than full, I applied for a Master's programme at a local seminary. I was going to become a professional Christian counsellor. It was in seminary that I gave God one last chance to fix the broken person that I was.

Promising myself to find healing, I spent days and months in the library researching anything I could find pertaining to human sexuality. If I could find the answers to fix my broken sexuality, I would surely help fix all of the other gays and lesbians in the world. But my research only led to more anger and self-hatred. After studying human development and sexuality, I was devastated to find an inherent process that all humans undergo. We are all born with a fixed temperament, a specific gene code, and a particular familial environment. My seminary professors used to claim that God had knit me in my mother's womb. With fury, I would question God. He knew the home in which I would be born. He knew what temperament I would have and the genes that would eventually express themselves. He had the master plan for who I would become. He set me up to be a damaged, broken boy and a failed sinner, and I had no choice in the matter. After sitting in counselling classes and reading several research articles in the library, I would drive home in rage. I would scream at God for picking me to be so despicable, especially when all I had ever craved to be was a valued, faithful son. I was not important to God. I would still burn in hell.

As faithful Christians, we are taught that we can control God's emotions with our behaviour. If we are moral and righteous, behaving perfectly, we will *keep* God happy. If we sin, we make God mad. Such a message is passed down from the pulpit to the congregation, from parents to children, and from seminary professor to graduating minister. We have created an illusion that it is only by our good behaviour that the almighty God remains pleased. What a backwards understanding of 'God is love' (1 John 4:8) we preach. In fact, in counselling psychology we call this the 'illusion of control' and it is one of the major pillars of codependency.

For most of my childhood, I practised the illusion of control as though it was my salvation. I believed that if I prayed every day, fasted two meals a day in high school, sang at church, read my Bible, and treated my neighbour with love that God would have no choice but to reward me by taking away my attractions for men. When the illusion had finally proved itself as a farce, I was incredibly relieved.

When we live as someone who internalises the truth of their creative design, we drop the facades and we turn off our performances. We shed the illusion of control and begin speaking authentically with the actions of our lives. We are not ashamed to show just how God intentionally wove our personhood into being. We are confident and steadfast because we understand that reflecting God and expressing God's creativity means being our most authentic self for all time in front of all people.

Section 1: Rejection

It was during a car ride home from seminary with angry tears falling down my face that I realised something. If God is love – the experience, development, feeling, and expression of love – then there cannot be a clean version of God and a dirty version of God. In other words, if God *is* love there is not a righteous version of love and a sinful version of love. Every form of *love* has to be God. I began to trust that my love was pure, no matter to whom it was directed and no matter from whom it was given. When I fell in love, with a man or a woman, I was experiencing and expressing God.

Several years later, I began to realise, as a faithful Christian, seminary professor, professional counsellor, and a devoted follower of Christ, that I was intentionally woven in my mother's womb after all (Psalms 139:13). God wanted me in that home, with this temperament, and these genes! My love wasn't dirty. I was supposed to be this man. No longer do I hear the echoing panic of nails trapping my personality into a coffin of self-hatred. I am free to show up just as God intends.

You see, it is not our job to convince God into loving us. It is God's desire to convince us that we are loved – for who we are, not who we can become. This is the opposite of the illusion of control and we call it unconditional love.

You Belong

Avery Belyeu

Avery Belyeu is a transgender educator, suicide prevention practitioner, and aspiring theologian. She is a second-year Master of Divinity student and Haggard Legacy Fellow at Brite Divinity School. She's a national expert on LGBTQ youth, suicide prevention, and youth homelessness. She has worked at the Trevor Project and currently works for a national suicide prevention organisation based in Washington, D.C. Avery currently serves on the advisory boards for the Runaway and Homeless Youth Training and Technical Assistance Center as well as Trans Lifeline, a suicide prevention lifeline serving the needs of the transgender community.

'God, please, please help me not be gay.' I said that prayer, or some variation of it, on an almost daily basis starting at around twelve years old. I prayed it when I went to bed at night, and when I woke up in the morning, and oftentimes in the middle of the day. Sometimes I even prayed it silently to myself as I sat next to my family on Sunday morning at the local Kingdom Hall of Jehovah's Witnesses. Sometimes I even thought about trying to make a bargain with God – I mean we have examples of that in the Bible, right? 'So, God, I will do anything you want me to for the rest of my life if you just help me not be gay. Anything.'

43

Eventually I stopped praying. I don't remember when it happened exactly. It was more of a slow gradual process, I think. I didn't stop being involved with my local congregation of Jehovah's Witnesses though. To the contrary I was more active than ever. At sixteen, I became a regular pioneer, an appointed position given to someone who spends 70 hours a month evangelising in the local community. And at eighteen I was appointed as a ministerial servant, the equivalent of a deacon in many other churches, and I gave my first Sunday sermon to a packed church. Looking back, I think that I felt that if I did everything just right, if I was the model young person, then God would eventually fix whatever this thing was that was wrong with me.

But it didn't work out that way. As the years went by the depression and feelings of loneliness and isolation increased. I couldn't find a way to reconcile the teachings of my congregation and the things I believed to be true with who I was deep inside. I felt like a liar. A fake. A fraud. Those feelings eventually brought me, at twenty-two years old, to the side of a mountain on the Blue Ridge Parkway, right outside West Jefferson, North Carolina. I pulled up to one of the mountain overlooks and sat on the side of a rocky ledge looking down at the green rolling hills thousands of feet below me. I had decided I was going to jump. Because I had really tried everything and I still wasn't any different than when I said that first prayer at twelve years old. And I knew that if my congregation found out I would be disfellowshipped. I'd lose my Church family, and worse than that I would lose my parents and my siblings too. My family would be disgraced, ashamed, and embarrassed and so disappointed in me. So, I decided to jump. It was just going to be easier that way.

But then I decided to pray. Just one last time I would pray. Looking back now this is when I remember that I hadn't prayed in a really long time. Starting that prayer felt like trying to start the engine of an old rusty car. It wasn't easy. But I looked out across the mountains and I prayed, 'God, I know we haven't talked in a long time, but listen I really need you to show up right now. And I don't just need a pat on the head. I need more than that – OK? I know you don't do signs or anything anymore but I really need something here. I need to know that you don't hate me for being who I am.' And as I prayed these words I looked over to my left and a deer and a fawn came walking out of the woods. They walked up so close I could have touched them. Then they froze and just looked at me with their big brown eyes. In my mind, the meaning was immediate. It was as if I heard God speak and say, 'I couldn't ever hate you any more than this deer could hate this little fawn. You are perfectly made. I love you just the way you are. And you are a part of all of this. You belong here.' Slowly, the deer and the fawn turned around and went back into the woods. I sat there for a few moments, stunned, and then I got up, got in my car and drove back down the mountain.

That day was just the start of a very long journey. I did come out and I was disowned by my family and rejected by my Church and the extended family that represented. The following few years were hard. Very hard. For a while I said I was agnostic, then atheist. No matter what I said though, in my heart I was always tethered to what happened on the side of the mountain that day. I knew that my journey with faith wasn't done. Eventually I found my way to an Episcopal Church. And it was in that place that I found community again. I was healed by the balm of the Eucharist and the rhythm of the liturgy calmed my mind and comforted my heart. I received masterful pastoral care from a wonderful and caring priest. And most importantly I learned how to pray again.

Eventually I found my way into suicide prevention as a line of work. And that was when I learned that my experience of feeling hopeless and alone isn't unique for young LGBTQ people – and sadly those feelings are often worse for young people in religious homes. I learned that LGBTQ youth are four times more likely to attempt suicide than straight youth. And young people who experience severe family rejection like I did are eight times more likely than their fellow LGBTQ peers to attempt suicide. I also learned that LGBTQ youth make up a staggering 40 per cent of the youth homeless population in the US. The research told me why, and told me how many, but it didn't have to tell me how any of this felt because I already knew. I lived it.

A few years after I started my career in suicide prevention I was living in New York City, and travelling a lot for work. My travels took me to a rural college in the South where I facilitated a workshop about LGBTQ folks and suicide prevention. A lot of the college students in the room were very emotional during the presentation. Many of them were having a hard time coming out. At the end of the presentation, a young woman came up to me and told me her story. With tears running down her face she described her struggle of coming out to her religious family. I knew what she was going through. I reached out and put my hand on her shoulder and said the words that I'd heard that day on the mountainside, 'You are perfectly made and God loves you just as you are.' She looked up at me a little stunned and said, 'No one has ever said that to me before. Thank you!' I think it was at that moment I knew that at some point in the future I would have to find a way to merge my suicide prevention career with church ministry.

Fast forward about five years and I came out again. After years of processing, I finally found the courage to declare that gay isn't really the right word to describe who I am and I came out fully as a transgender woman. But this time coming out was different. This time I had a community of people surrounding me who are companions on this new journey; companions who know how important it is to look deep into my eyes and tell me, 'You are beautiful. You are perfectly made. God loves you exactly as you are.' My journey has also taken me to a progressive seminary where I am learning to integrate my passion for public health and mental health with sound theology: theology that liberates and heals.

And I have begun to form a new prayer that I pray almost daily but it's a prayer that's so different than the prayer I began to pray when I was twelve years old. I pray for a Church that will put the law of love before doctrines about gender and sexuality. I pray for a Church that will open its arms wide and embrace the outcast, and care for the wounded. I lift up my hands and I pray for all the young LGBTQ people who are trying to discern how to reconcile who they know they are with what they hear from the pulpit each Sunday. I pray for them to have hope, courage, and resilience no matter what may come. And I pray that, if and when those young LGBTQ folks face the hardship of rejection from their Church and family, there will be a church on every corner that opens its doors wide to care for the wounded, to pray for healing, and to look deeply into the eyes of that young person and say, 'You are beautiful, you are perfectly made. God loves you *exactly* as you are. You are welcome here. You are part of all of this. You belong.'

From Death to Life

Jennifer Hoffman

Jennifer has recently relocated to California, where she now works as a Service Coordinator and Youth Program Leader at Palo Alto Housing. Prior to her relocation, she was a Certified Tobacco Treatment Specialist and Prevention Specialist for three years for Pittsburgh Mercy Health System in Pittsburgh, Pennsylvania. During her time in Pittsburgh, she also created LOCO Fitness, a venture that was designed to create an environment conducive to physical and spiritual growth. Jennifer's passion and desire to grow as a person translates into the relationships she builds with the children and adults she works with on a daily basis. In April 2017, Jennifer's passion of creating authentic spaces for people to share their truth gave her the opportunity to speak at TEDx Texas A&M. Her talk was titled 'Authentic Truth Requires Authentic Spaces'.

Throughout my four years in high school, I would have recurring dreams about dying. While they weren't always the same dream, they always had one of two themes. Sometimes I would die in a car accident, skidding off the road during a winter storm, hitting a tree or telephone pole. Other times I would be floating above my own funeral. These dreams happened so frequently and were so potent I started to believe that I wasn't going to live for very long. Somewhere along the way, I had made up

49

in my brain that twenty-five years old would be the end mark of my existence, though, at the time, I had no idea why that number seemed relevant.

I grew up in a Catholic household, not because we were strictly practising, but because my father grew up in a Catholic home. To this day, my grandparents, who are in their nineties, still attend Mass twice a week. I'm fairly certain my mother wanted us to follow in the same path, not because she was an overly religious person, but because she grew up with an atheist father. My mother never really speaks of God or faith. However, she has the word 'Believe' sprinkled all around my parents' house as if leaving silent notes of love and faith for all to see. My entire life, I have subconsciously known nothing but to hope and believe in something greater, something higher. Maybe that belief is from all her sprinkling; maybe it has been the way my soul craves to know myself and what's around me deeper than what the eyes can see. When I look back at my life, everything looks so much more intentional. I can see the way God has had His hands on me and moved through my life. What seems coincidental in our lives always carries a deeper meaning in purpose. We just don't recognise them until later.

I was baptised, received my first communion, and confirmed in a small Catholic church in my also very small hometown. I won't lie – I hated catechism. I didn't understand the stories because I couldn't relate to them. I always felt like I was being talked at, told what to do, what to believe, what to say, when to stand, when to kneel, and everything else in between. I have nothing against Catholicism. I have not a single doubt in my mind that everything God does is intentional. However, at the time, I wasn't interested. By the end of high school, prayer became this superficial use of making wishes to God as if

He were a genie. Simultaneously, I was starting to realise that what I thought was looking up to women because they were good at the sports I was playing was actually much more than that. The details of how and who helped me find that out are irrelevant. However, the story of my first girlfriend is one of confusion, heartbreak, and absolute fear of anyone finding out. It was, without a doubt, one of the loneliest and most frightening times in my life. Much of why I am who I am – and why I find it necessary for us all to own our stories and authentic truth. To hold space for people to own their truth unapologetically by holding a space where that fear and confusion won't be experienced in my presence.

To be clear, prior to my first girlfriend in high school, I didn't know what gay was. All I knew of being gay was Puck from *The Real World* and what I overheard adults saying about it being a sin in my Church. One day, my girlfriend completely stopped talking to me – no warning, no letter, no explanation. To this day I have no idea what happened. We passed each other in the halls, had gym lockers next to each other, and saw each other at parties. However, after that day she never said a single word to me. I have never been in that darkness and fear since that time during my senior year in high school. Asking who I was, what does that even mean, and not having a single person I felt comfortable enough to tell my story to. This is where I began to question if there could be a God at all. I was flooded with questions to this genie up above: who would create me like this knowing the fear and pain I would live in daily? How did you make a mistake with me? Why is it so wrong to love another human, regardless of their gender or identity?

For the following seven years through college and a graduate programme, the God of my catechism days became nothing more than a 'higher power' that I believed used karma to deliver or restrict our lives. I believed bad things happened to good people because good people would use their pain, their weaknesses, their struggles, and their darkest days as a catalyst for change. I didn't know *who* or *what* that higher power was, but I knew something was running this controlled chaos that I saw of the world.

Shortly after I finished grad school, I started dating a woman who loved God in ways that made absolutely no sense to me. She was strong in her faith. Her church community was nothing like what I understood of religion. The love that burned inside her for God turned everything I made my world of 'faith' into upside down. For the first time in my life, my mother sprinkling 'Believe' around our house finally made sense when I heard my girlfriend talk about her faith. It was a handful of days before my twenty-fifth birthday, and I asked this woman, who had given me a new meaning of religion, 'How could God ever love me if I'm gay?' She took my hands and told me, 'Sweetheart, you are not a mistake. God has never stopped loving you. All He has made you to be is out of love, and there is never a mistake in that.' In that moment, the incessant dreams about death came true. I died when I turned twenty-five, because when those words spilled out of her mouth, it was the first time in my twenty-four years on this planet that I heard God. I was reborn.

Since then, my life has been an endless wandering through the wondering of all these questions – never because I didn't know who I was, but from realising my entire life, we are all constantly unfolding who we are and what we believe in. Faith and coming out are not destinations, but a journey to be lived through love and grace, and a journey that opens us up more and more to our truest and most authentic selves. Faith has been like my coming out story – ongoing, constantly transforming, and always renewing with every experience and every human soul I encounter.

The Exorcism

Billy Kluttz

Billy Kluttz works as Director of Music at Church of the Pilgrims (PCUSA) in Washington, D.C. and Evening Service Co-ordinator at Immanuel Presbyterian Church (USA) in McLean, Virginia. He is passionate about creative liturgy and worship, country and bluegrass music, and the role of technology in the emerging church and non-profit sector.

Like many people, my journey to reconcile faith and identity began with an exorcism.

I grew up in a conservative Evangelical Christian family in the south-eastern US. My parents were good and loving people – despite our differences of opinion on several matters of importance – but more on that later.

Decisions about my faith and identity arrived during high school. I came out to my mother at age sixteen in the upstairs of our suburban North Carolina home; it did not go well. I remember struggling to get the words out. I remember my mother on the floor, devastated and crying after I told her that I was gay. My only request was that she not tell my father when he got home; minutes later, she told him the news as he walked in the door.

That's when the exorcism happened. It wasn't one of the exciting, Hollywood-type exorcisms that you see on TV, the ones with spinning heads and well-trained priests. Rather, it was a sort of do-it-yourself, old-fashioned exorcism. Believing that an otherworldly force had convinced me that I was gay, my parents laid hands on me and prayed vigorously for Satan to leave my body. They attempted to cast out demons while I lay there on the floor.

That night, I realised that I was never going to have a typical coming out story, a cute anecdote you can share during small talk and first dates. But that night, on the floor of my childhood home, waiting for the prayers and tears to end, something changed.

I found Jesus that night, face down in the carpet of my childhood home. I heard the loud prayers above me, asking God to heal and forgive me. I heard the shouts of anger and sadness. But I also heard another voice simply saying, 'No.' Above the commotion, I heard a voice telling me, 'No. Don't believe it. Don't listen to this. Enough.'

My journey towards self-acceptance did not take years of intense study and prayer. For me, reconciliation was not the result of the perfect logical argument or well-constructed syllogism. That's not my story.

My story is a relational one. I found Jesus during an exorcism. It was God's Holy 'No' that saved my life that night.

It is that same Holy Negation that keeps many LGBT+ folks alive. The taunts of street preachers, the distance of friends, the silence of family holiday dinners, are survived only because of God's still, small voice saying, 'No. This is ridiculous. Tune this out.'

During seminary, I learned that there is a grand theological term for all of this sacred naysaying: apophatic theology. Apophatic, or negative, theology begins by describing what God is not in order to approach what God is.

It's great to have an academic term, but I still prefer 'God's Holy No'.

It takes years (perhaps decades) of faithfully saying no before you can ever say yes; this is the first great truth of queer Christianity. The ancient Christian confessions ask us to begin with a long list of affirmations; queer Christians begin, instead, with our own liturgy of negation.

We say no to communities of hurt and harm. We reject theologies of transphobia, heterosexism, and cissexism. Maybe most difficult of all, we slowly learn to silence the sounds of self-hatred and doubt deep within our own souls.

Our theological story is one of tearing down and rebuilding. I think that is what excites me most about our moment in the Church's history. After a generation of faithful negation and survival, we are on the cusp of a Great Queer Yes. We are on the verge of a new affirmation of faith that is just now breaking into voice, symbol, and sign.

I see this in the movement toward LGBT+ inclusion in a growing number of Christian denominations. I feel this in communities of faith taking up the calling to work against LGBT+ bullying and homelessness. I sense this as we work together to craft new liturgies for our shared life: celebrating gender transitions, same-gender weddings, coming out stories, and more. Perhaps most powerfully, I see this affirmation at work in my own family.

Fortunately, our family's story did not end with an exorcism; it was only our beginning. The exorcism allowed us to begin casting out demons of other sorts.

In truth, we learned to say no together to the harmful theologies at work in our lives. It wasn't easy, but it was profoundly healing. We kept talking and learning together even when our theologies, opinions, and core convictions collided.

The horrible thing about grace is that even our enemies get the same kind treatment.

There wasn't a lot of grace in our family when I came out. There wasn't a lot of grace in our family when my brother, my only other sibling, came out a year later (to a similarly warm reception). The Church that raised me rejected me and a few months afterward, my brother went through the same judgement and sanction.

Grace's insistence on equal access is hard to come to terms with, but its contagion is awe-inspiring. That's what my family learned. We learned that a little bit of grace was a dangerous thing. It wasn't about convincing my parents in an argument; it wasn't about debating the finer points of Greek or Hebrew translations; and it certainly wasn't about their hermeneutics and exegetical perspectives.

Instead, it was about an exorcism, albeit of a different sort. One where grace came in and threw out our collective games of guilt, retribution, and you'll get what's coming the next time around. That was a beautiful thing to watch.

For our family, it looked like my parents finally forgiving themselves for a lot of things: past marriages, personal shortcomings, their own doubts. For my brother and me, it was learning a radical self-love that allowed us to heal; it was finding a new kind of forgiveness for those who had wounded us even as they tried to love us.

That's the Jesus that I found that night, face down in the carpet, amid an exorcism and everything else. A Jesus that showed up with a Holy No, ready to move in with grace and new dishes. I believe that our family has continued to meet Jesus along our collective journey.

And, together, we have learned to say no and to listen anew.

It hasn't been about being right or winning points in a culture war. For us, it has been about the merciful grace of God that keeps showing up during exorcisms and the most unlikely of places to say enough, drop the stones, there's a better way.

Dear Church

Brandan Robertson

Brandan Robertson is the author of Nomad: A Spirituality
For Travelling Light *(DLT Books, 2016) and writes regularly
for* Patheos *and the* Huffington Post. *He is the founder
and Executive Director of Nomad Partnerships, a non-
profit working to foster spiritual and social evolution around
the world. He served as the immediate past national
spokesperson of Evangelicals for Marriage Equality and has
served on the US State Department's Working Group on
Religion and LGBT+ Rights and the Democratic National
Convention's LGBT+ Advisory Board. Brandan earned
his Bachelor's degree in pastoral ministry and theology
from Moody Bible Institute and his Master of Theological
Studies from Iliff School of Theology.*

Dear Church,

Hello. It's Me.

You know. The heretic. The one who walked away. The
backslider.

Hello from the other side.

You know. I've loved you for a long time. Ever since I
was twelve years old, when I walked down the aisle of
the old Baptist church.

I didn't have an ounce of hope in my soul. At the time,
I was the son of an abusive alcoholic father. I grew up in a

trailer park where a vision for the future wasn't our focus. We were just hoping to get to next week.

At twelve, I was crushed. I had no plans for my life. I felt worthless. But as I made my way down that aisle and fell to my knees at that altar, tears washing down my face as the congregation was singing

> Just as I am without one plea
> But that thy blood was shed for me
> And that thou bidd'st me come to thee
> Oh Lamb of God, I come, I come.

I felt a love so powerful. So transformative, so redemptive, from a Heavenly Father who loved me more than my earthly father ever could. I heard a Gospel that was truly good news for my young soul. I felt, for the first time, the spark of hope. I believed, for the first time, that my life had a purpose, had a meaning.

Dear Church, you have shown me so much love. You've formed me. You've made me into the man I am today.

It was just a few months after that experience with God, I sat in my backyard reading the Bible and I felt a gentle yet powerful tug at my heart. I sensed God calling me. Calling me to be a pastor. To give my life to serve his Church. To preach his word. To bring the love and hope that I had found in Jesus to the world around me. And ever since then, that's been the focus of my life.

Dear Church, you taught me so much about what it is to be a follower of Jesus. I've seen your love poured out on me, like the time when dozens of people showed up at our dilapidated trailer unannounced, offering to do renovations, replacing floors, buying groceries, and handing a wad of money to us to help my struggling family get by for another week.

Section 1: Rejection

I've seen you reach out to people experiencing homelessness. I have seen you advocate on behalf of the voiceless. I have watched you preach the Gospel to the most lost and hopeless individuals, and I have seen new life spring forth because of you.

Dear Church, I've given my life to serve you. From internships, to Bible college, and seminary. Every ounce of my energy for the past decade has been given to preparing to teach you, to guide you, to give back to you all that you have given me. I love you and believe in you. I believe you have the power to transform the world.

Dear Church, my heart beats for you.

But something has happened recently and *everything seems to have changed*.

Dear Church, you taught me that I was created in the image and likeness of an eternally expansive, diverse, uncontainable, and indescribable God. Doesn't it make sense, then, that I would be unique, diverse... different? Doesn't that mean that we should not be seeking so much uniformity, but instead seeking out uniqueness?

So that when we come together as a whole, we make up a big, beautiful, diverse body that mirrors that image of God.

Why then, have you told me that I can no longer truly reflect the image of God because I'm queer? Where has the image of God gone? Isn't it still here? Don't I still bear it? Doesn't God delight in me, just as I am?

Or was that just part of the sales pitch?

Dear Church, why is it that, at the moment when I feel most truly authentic and most truly connected to God, you have pushed me away and said I am invalid? Why must who I am as a person cause you to fear me so much? Since when did I become such a problem?

When I kept my sexuality hidden, you lauded me. You told me I was anointed of God. That I was going to be used by God to change the world. Every week after Church dozens of older Church members would come up to me to tell me that they were so proud of me and knew that God's hand was on my life. Now, when I walk into that same church, I only get side glares and people telling me that they're 'praying for me'.

What's changed?

That I'm more honest? More authentic? More devoted to Christ than ever before? Yet nothing is the same between us. Instead of a beloved member of your community, *I'm a stranger and exile in the house of God*. The place where I once found a warm embrace has now become a place of rejection and scorn.

Dear Church, you tell me you only do this because you love me. But love doesn't check a person's sexuality or gender identity before embracing them. Yet, you tell me, *'This is only for your good'* and *'I just feel that God wants me to share this with you.'*

You look at me from across the table, or worse, from behind a computer screen, and lay out a case for just how deceived and dangerous I have become. I've received message after message that say things like, and I quote:

> Certainly you're a leader, Brandan. It is safe to say that in the current trajectory of your life you will usher many into a hellish existence. And when you need the blood of Christ to wash away your sins, where will you turn, now that you have renounced His redeeming and transforming work so thoroughly? But I already know, you have a victim mentality and you use

your sense of victimhood to victimize others. Your behavior is repugnant to me.

Comments like this are not random. They come from former friends, mentors, pastors. Message after message, you shame me. Rebuke me. Condemn me. Without ever actually talking to me. Asking about my life. You assume the worst. You seem to no longer care for me as a person. Only that I renounce my honesty and return to the shadows of your theological perspective.

No one should have to face such condemnation. Especially from those who bear the name of the Christ who proclaimed, *'I have not come to condemn, but to redeem'*.

Dear Church, much to your surprise, I still have a deep relationship with God. I still read the Bible. I love the Bible. Good grief, I'm even working on a second degree in the Bible and theology.

I know what this book says. I know what God wants for me. And just because we've come to different conclusions about how I live my life and serve our God doesn't mean that I need to be your next evangelistic effort. There can be space at the table of God's grace for both of us. Christ heals divisions. He calls us to set aside our differences – yes, even differences about what is or is not sin.

Dear Church, don't you believe the words of Scripture?

Don't you believe what the Apostle Paul wrote in the Letter to the Romans:

> Who are you to judge another person's servants? So stop judging each other. Instead, never put a stumbling block or obstacle in the way of your brother or sister. God's kingdom isn't about what one person thinks is unclean and what another thinks isn't, but about

righteousness, joy, and peace in the Holy Spirit.
So let's strive for the things that bring peace and
the things that build each other up.

Dear Church, why have you slammed your door in my face? Will you heed Paul's word?

Dear Church, didn't Jesus say that we shall know true disciples by their fruit? Have you heard these stories? Do you see these lives? We're passionately giving ourselves over to God for the good of our world. Our lives are overflowing with love, and joy, and peace, and patience, and… well, you know the list. Why, then, are you so quick to invalidate our salvation?

How could I have been saved so profoundly just one year ago and now be considered unclean? Has the cross of Christ become weakened? Has the power of his resurrection come up deficient?

Dear Church, please explain to me how my sexuality has become a 'Gospel' issue. Since when has the announcement of God's Kingdom and salvation through Christ ever been based upon what gender somebody falls in love with? Please tell me how disagreement about the interpretation of six verses out of over 30,000 in the Bible have come to represent the 'greatest threat to the Church' today?

Dear Church, what are you so afraid of? Doesn't the perfect love of Christ cast out all fear? Dear Church, where is your love?

Dear Church, don't you believe in the power of the living and active word of God?

Dear Church, believe it or not, it's not in spite of, but *because* of the Word that I have decided to 'come out' as queer. It's precisely because I believe that God is still speaking to us and that the Kingdom of heaven is in our midst that I fight for the rights of my LGBT+ siblings in society and in the Church.

Dear Church, we're not an issue. We're not imaginary. We are queer followers of Jesus and we are *here*. We have a voice. We are committed to the radical, self-sacrificial way of Jesus, our Lord. And while I know that our existence doesn't fit in your theological paradigm, *it is reality*. And when reality and theology clash, *it's probably time to rethink your theology*. When your theology pushes people away from God, from hope, from life, something has gone terribly wrong. When shame, self-hatred, and fear is the result of your teaching, you can be assured that your words are not from God.

Dear Church, even in the midst of all of this, I still have grace for you. God has chosen to make up his Kingdom of beautifully broken people among whom I am the chief. I know that many of you have the best intentions. You really do want to do what's right. To stand on the truth. To love me in the way that you believe God demands. I have been sitting in your seat. I too struggled to accept LGBT+ people. To accept myself. I understand your struggle. I've been there too. It took a lot of work. A lot of time. A lot of prayer. A lot of openness to the Holy Spirit to stand where I am today.

And that's all I am asking of you today.

Not to change your mind overnight. But to be humble. Make room in your life to learn. To rethink. To ask hard questions. To listen to and accept the stories that make you feel uncomfortable. Do it, not because your life needs to centre around this topic, but because of the fact that there *are* people in your life, in your faith community, that are LGBT+. I guarantee it. Do it because Christ commands it of you. Do it because *every person matters to God*. Do it because *real* lives are on the line. Do it because the Gospel of Jesus calls us to sacrifice our comfort, our privilege, and our power for the good of the other. The least of these. The minority.

In that way, I guess, this is, in fact a Gospel issue.

Because if the Gospel you proclaim isn't good news to the poor, liberation to the captive, recovery of sight to the blind, and God's ridiculous grace *for all*, then it isn't the Gospel of Jesus. It's, by definition, a false Gospel.

This Kingdom is a kingdom for misfits. For minorities. For queers. For the outcasts. For those who don't seem to belong. This Kingdom is a kingdom for all who reflect the image and likeness of God. And I've got news for you. That means *all of us.*

Dear Church, LGBT+ people *are already* the Church. You don't have the power to exclude us from participating in Christ. The table, the Kingdom, and the power is God's and God's alone. And he has welcomed us in.

Dear Church, God is doing a new thing in our day. God is decentralising those who have held power and privilege in his name for too long. A revival is breaking forth. Droves are finding renewed life in the way of Christ. Our voice is getting louder. Our influence is gaining strength. And our agenda, well, it's simple:

> To see the Kingdom of this world transformed
> into the Kingdom of our Lord and of his Christ.

To see justice roll forth like a river. Equity and peace on every corner of the earth. It's to embody the Spirit of Christ to our world.

And that's a dangerous agenda, indeed. For it challenges the systems of power and oppression in our world. It threatens to unhinge all that we've built to make our lives comfortable. But it's an unstoppable one.

And to my LGBT+ siblings, let me say it again. We are already the Church. We don't need to wait to be included. We already are. Just as we are.

We *are* the Body of Christ.

We *are* included in the Kingdom of God.

We *do* bear the image and likeness of God.

We are *not* broken.

We must stand strong, and live into our calling to be ambassadors of Christ and his reconciling message to our world. We must refuse to return evil for evil, judgement for judgement. We must embody grace, patience, and forgiveness. But that doesn't mean we stay *silent*.

We must open our mouths. Open our hearts. Open our lives. And let the light of Christ within us shine forth, so that the world can see our good works and glorify God because of us. We are *the* channels of renewal and revival. We are the future.

May we not grow proud or resentful. May we instead seek to embody both grace and truth. Because truth will win out. Grace will win out. Love will win out in the end. I guarantee it.

Dear Church, here we are. *This is our witness*.

SECTION 2:
RECONCILIATION

The foundational beliefs of the Christian faith are often summarised in what the writers of the New Testament call 'the Gospel'. This word 'gospel' comes from the Greek εὐαγγέλιον (euaggelion), which literally means, 'to bring good news'. This word 'gospel' appears dozens of times throughout the New Testament, and is used to refer to the message that Jesus himself came to proclaim and embody, containing the keys to salvation for humankind. To begin thinking about the metanarrative of Christian theology, there is no more essential place to start than here. Throughout the biblical texts themselves and Christian theology through the ages, there is much variance in what exactly the message of the Gospel is. For our purposes, I will root my understanding in the definition that the writer of the Gospel of Mark has Jesus speaking, because many biblical scholars agree that Mark's gospel contains some of the most reliable quotes from Jesus, based on earlier source texts.[1] In chapter one of the gospel, the author of Mark says:

1   For more on the Marcan priority theory, see Mark Goodacre, *The Synoptic Problem: A Way Through the Maze* (London, T&T Clark, 2001), pp. 20–23.

> Jesus came into Galilee announcing God's good
> news, saying: 'Now is the time! Here comes
> God's Kingdom! Change your hearts and lives,
> and trust this good news!'[2]

According to this passage, the 'good news' that Jesus preached was quite concise and simple: it is the announcement that the Kingdom of God was coming and an invitation to change our hearts and lives to trust in the emerging reality of that Kingdom. Throughout the rest of Jesus' teachings as portrayed in the synoptic gospels, he repeats this message about the arrival of the Kingdom of God over and over again. The Gospel according to Jesus is about this new reality he called the Kingdom of God, and therefore, this must be the foundation of all Christian theology and practice.

What, then, is the Kingdom of God, and what impact might it have on our understanding of the inclusion of sexual and gender minorities in the life of the Church? To answer this question, we turn to the words of the Apostle Paul in his Letter to the Romans where Paul writes: 'For the kingdom of God is... justice, and peace, and joy in the Holy Spirit.'[3] In this statement, Paul, writing to the Church at Rome in the midst of great conflict over how to observe Jewish laws and customs, suggests that the Kingdom of God is not some far-off, supernatural reality, but rather a Spirit-led movement of justice, peace, and joy – realities that should be experienced in the life of the Church and in the world here and now.

Theologian Jürgen Moltmann builds on Paul's definition, suggesting that the Kingdom of God is a present, tangible reality, brought and demonstrated in the person of Jesus

2   Mark 1:14–15, *Common English Bible*.
3   Romans 14:17.

himself, as well as a spiritual reality, described as an ever-deepening union with God. Moltmann writes:

> [The] Kingdom of God – that means God is near and present and allows God's creatures to participate in God's attributes, in God's glory and beauty, in God's vivacity and God's goodness, because at the same time God participates in the attributes of God's creatures, in their finiteness, in their vulnerability, and in their morality. (I John 4:6)... The Church is not there for its own sake but rather for the 'concern of Jesus.' All inherent interest of the Church itself... must be subordinated to the interests of the Kingdom of God... The divine mission of the Church consists [of] bringing the oppressed their freedom, the humiliated their human dignity, and those without rights their rights... [We must] participate in the Kingdom of God and today let something from the rebirth of all things become visible which Christ will complete on his day.[4]

Moltmann, echoing the words of both Paul and Jesus, furthers our understanding that the Kingdom of God must be understood to be a present and growing reality of union with God, resulting in the expansion of justice, peace, and equity for all of God's creatures. According to Jesus, in his many parables about the Kingdom of God, it is both a present reality and one that continues to grow and progress. When Jesus speaks of the Kingdom, he likens it to leaven in dough[5] and a mustard seed planted

4   Jürgen Moltmann, 'Jesus and the Kingdom of God', *The Asbury Theological Journal* 48 (1993), 5–18.
5   Matthew 13:33.

in a field.[6] The imagery used here is one of gradual growth and expansion, requiring human effort to knead the dough and cultivate the seeds that are planted. Another way to understand this is that Jesus, in his life, planted the seeds of the Kingdom. He demonstrated in his own actions what it looks like to live in step with the Kingdom of God, or the world as God intends it to be. He then left it up to his disciples to cultivate the seeds so that the Kingdom of God would grow and expand throughout the earth as the reality of justice and equity for all people.

To be a disciple of Jesus is to be one who 'changes your heart and life and trusts'[7] in the path that Jesus demonstrated. According to the teachings of the gospels, this is what will bring ultimate wholeness to our world. But as we clearly see throughout the entire life of Jesus, his path is not an easy or convenient one to follow. It requires humility, sacrifice, and selflessness. It shouldn't be surprising to us, then, that a majority of what is sold as 'Christianity' in our world has little to do with this message of liberation and equality for all people, but one that has been abstracted by theological musings and understood to be about a supernatural salvation in the afterlife, with little influence on the world we live in now.

If the message at the heart of Christianity is a message of an ever-expanding reality of justice and equality for societies most marginalised and oppressed, then that must be the starting point for any conversation pertaining to inclusion in the Church. As prominent black liberation theologian James Cone notes:

> Any view of the gospel that fails to understand the Church as that community whose work and

6   Matthew 13:31–2.
7   Mark 1:15.

consciousness are defined by the community of the oppressed is not Christian and is thus heretical.[8]

In Cone's understanding, unless the message that is preached and embodied by Christian communities fully reflects the life and teaching of Jesus and his preferential option for the poor, marginalised, and oppressed of society, then it cannot be accepted as true Christianity.

This understanding of the Gospel has roots in the teachings of Jesus himself and has been a common understanding throughout Christian history. From the early patristic writings[9] through the abolitionist movements of the eighteenth century,[10] the liberationist movement of the early twentieth century,[11] and the feminist movements of the mid twentieth century,[12] the idea that the message of Jesus was directed to society's most oppressed groups has undergirded Christian teaching for 2000 years. Any understanding of Christianity that lacks this liberationist undergirding, then, is failing to interpret the Gospel through the lens of Jesus and the writings of the gospels which cast Christ's entire mission and ministry in a liberationist light.

One major recurring theme in the synoptic gospels is that Jesus continually finds himself battling with the religious leaders of his day over his seeming disregard for the religious dogma derived from the Hebrew Bible. Over

---

8   James Cone, *God of the Oppressed* (New York, Orbis, 2000), p. 37.
9   J. Kameron Carter draws extensively on early Christian sources for liberation in his groundbreaking book, *Race: A Theological Account* (Oxford, Oxford University Press, 2008).
10 See the writings of William Wilberforce.
11 See the work of Gustavo Gutiérriez, Jon Sobrino, and James Cone.
12 See the work of Marie Maugeret, Elisabeth Schüssler Fiorenza, and Catherine Keller.

a dozen times throughout the written accounts,[13] the Pharisees and Sadducees are found confronting Jesus for his blatant disregard for biblical law or religious custom. Jesus, however, seems to take great delight in frustrating these religious leaders, offering new interpretations and further progressions on the laws of old. For instance, the Gospel of Matthew records a long series of teachings in which Jesus directly quotes from the Old Testament and then directly contradicts the commandment and raises the ethical standard. He begins his teaching by saying, 'Do not think that I have come to abolish the Law, but to fulfil it.'[14] The word, πληρῶσαι, which is translated 'fulfil' in many Bible translations of this verse, can also be translated as 'complete'. I believe that this translation helps us to understand what Jesus is trying to communicate in this teaching.

Progressive revelation is the belief that God reveals more and more truth over time, as humanity is able to receive and adopt the 'fullness of truth'. In the Christian tradition, Jesus is understood to be the embodiment of the fullness of truth, the example of what a life lived in accordance with the will of God looks like. As the writer of the Letter to the Hebrews says, 'In the past, God spoke through the prophets to our ancestors in many times and many ways. In these final days, though, he has spoken to us through his Son.'[15] Jesus is seen as the supreme revelation of God to earth, in whom 'the fullness of God was pleased to dwell'.[16] His words, then, are seen to be the completion and truest embodiment of many of the

---

13 For a sampling of these confrontations, see Matthew 15:1; 16:1–6; 23:1–4; Luke 11:37; 14:3.
14 Matthew 5:17.
15 Hebrews 1:1–2.
16 Colossians 1:19.

Hebrew Bible's commands, which were only partially or incompletely revealed.

In Matthew 5, we witness Jesus building upon laws from the Hebrew Bible and bringing them to a more complete and holistic ethical standard. For instance, he says:

> You have heard that it was said, 'An eye for an eye and a tooth for a tooth.' But I say to you that you must not oppose those who hurt you. If people slap you on your right cheek, you must turn the left cheek to them as well.[17]

Jesus quotes directly from Exodus 21:24, and then significantly amends the commandment, raising the ethical standard. Now, his disciples aren't permitted to retaliate, but are commanded to embrace non-violent resistance as the norm. The ethic has been altered, the standard has been raised. Jesus renders the old law irrelevant in light of his new law, rooted in unconditional love. Jesus does this six times over the course of Matthew 5, each time taking a biblical commandment and amending it to be more ethical and just.

Jesus clearly has no problem amending Scripture. He clearly is not working from a paradigm of biblical inerrancy. For Jesus, the Bible is a living text, always evolving and always being brought nearer to 'completion'. This makes sense when one realises that even the rabbis of old viewed the Scriptures as texts to be reinterpreted, revised, and reconfigured based on the current era and context that they found themselves in. This tradition was known as midrash, which is described by Hebrew literature scholar Dr David Stern in the following way:

17 Matthew 5:38–9.

> [Midrash is] a specific name for the activity of
> biblical interpretation as practiced by the Rabbis
> of the land of Israel in the first five centuries of
> the common era... By the end of the biblical
> period, the locus for [the search for God's will]
> appears to have settled on the text of the Torah
> where, it was now believed, God's will for the
> present moment was to be found.[18]

In other words, midrash was a traditional rabbinical
method, which relied upon the written text of the Torah
to find wisdom and guidance for the present moment.
This resulted in texts being taken out of their original
context (*the* chief sin among Evangelical theologians)
and applied to situations which the original author would
never have even considered. But this was how Scripture
was to be used. As a channel through which the Spirit
of God could illumine old wisdom for new circumstance,
resulting in new interpretations, new ideas, and even new
additions to and subtractions from the biblical text. A few
centuries after the initial writing of the Torah, the rabbis
were already reinterpreting some of the strict commands
of the Torah in order to make life more reasonable and
practical for the average Jewish person. Throughout
history, the biblical texts were seen as 'living and active'[19]
and not static and unchanging. This is how Jesus viewed
the texts himself, bringing many of the existing ethical
interpretations of laws from the Hebrew Bible to their
completion through consideration of those on the margins.
To many, this looked like transgression of the law, and
indeed, it was. But in transgressing one version of the law,

18 Adele Berlin and David Stern, *Jewish Study Bible* (Oxford, Oxford University
Press, 2004), p. 1864.
19 Hebrews 4:12.

Jesus revealed a higher standard for his disciples to live by. Biblical scholar Dr Cheryl Anderson notes that:

> Jesus violated [traditional] standards to reincorporate those who had been excluded… the inclusive table fellowship of Jesus stands in stark contrast to the exclusive table fellowship of the Pharisees.[20]

Furthermore, Jesus makes it clear that God's revelatory work will not cease with him. Indeed, he tells his disciples that the Holy Spirit would continue her revelatory work indefinitely. Jesus says to his disciples, 'I still have much to tell you, but you cannot yet bear to hear it. However, when the Spirit of truth comes, [it] will guide you into all the truth.'[21] In other words, as Jesus is looking towards his nearing death, he tells the disciples that there is much more that he desires for them to know, but doesn't believe they are able to bear it at the present time. This is a fundamental Christian belief – that God has (and will) reveal truth progressively, over time, as humanity is able to 'bear' or comprehend it. As reformed Evangelical theologian Dr Vern Poythress writes, describing progressive revelation:

> God did not say everything at once. The earlier communications take into account the limitations in the understanding of people at earlier times. The later communications build on the earlier.[22]

20 Cheryl Anderson, *Ancient Laws and Contemporary Controversies: The Need for Inclusive Biblical Interpretation* (Oxford, Oxford University Press, 2009), p. 92.
21 John 16:12–13.
22 Peter Lillback, Vern Poythress, Iain M. Duguid, G. K. Beale, and Richard B. Gaffin, *Seeing Christ in All of Scripture: Hermeneutics at Westminster Theological Seminary* (Philadelphia, PA, Westminster Seminary, 2016), p. 10.

God is still speaking. Though the biblical canon may be closed as a matter of tradition, the ongoing revelatory work of God clearly continues to unfold throughout human history, leading society towards higher ethical ideals of inclusion, equality, and wholeness. This reality has been and is currently experienced by followers of Christ throughout the ages and is completely aligned with the teachings and expectations of Jesus. If we are to be faithful to God in our present age, we must pay close attention to the nudges of the Spirit, gently calling us to step beyond our beliefs and traditions to widen the gates of the Kingdom of God.

Re-examining Biblical Texts: Exploring Inclusive Biblical Interpretation

When one examines the way that Jesus and the early Apostles used Scripture, we begin to see a clear trajectory towards higher ethical standards and a more inclusive vision for the Kingdom of God. In 2001, Evangelical theologian William Webb published a groundbreaking book[23] where he posited a hermeneutical lens for interpreting Scripture that he called 'the redemptive-movement hermeneutic'. This hermeneutic traced the redemptive trajectory of ethics from the Hebrew Bible to the New Testament, showing that ethical consciousness of society continually grew, albeit slowly, towards a more inclusive and equal posture for all people. Webb's hermeneutic argued that faithful Christians are called to move beyond the static words of Scripture, taking the 'spirit' of the words and applying them to our modern

---

23   William Webb, *Slaves, Women & Homosexuals: Exploring the Hermeneutics of Cultural Analysis* (Downers Grove, Intervarsity, 2001).

contexts to help us determine the faithful response to our ethical questions. Webb writes:

> Scripture does not present a 'finalized ethic' in every area of human relationship… to stop where the Bible stops (with its isolated words) ultimately fails to reapply the redemptive spirit of the text as it spoke to the original audience. It fails to see that further reformation is possible… While Scripture had a positive influence in its times, we should take that redemptive spirit and move to an even better, more fully-realized ethic today.[24]

Webb's argument opens the door for continued societal reform, based on the spirit of the biblical texts, rather than the static words themselves. And while Webb's 'redemptive-movement hermeneutic' was groundbreaking for the Evangelical world in 2001, it is hardly a new idea or concept. Instead, it has been clearly demonstrated in the field of biblical interpretation[25] and in the texts themselves for thousands of years. As we noted earlier, feminist and liberationist theologians have relied on ethical trajectories in Scripture and the cultural context of the writer as the interpretive keys to unlock the liberating power of the biblical text. Feminist theologian Carol Lakey Hess notes:

> [Biblical] texts… reflect the prevailing cultural ethos… we must use these to recognize that the Biblical writers were human persons immersed in – though not limited to – the language, mores,

24 Webb, *Slaves, Women & Homosexuals*, p. 247.
25 Similar theological arguments have been made by a wide array of theologians in the modern era such as J. R. Daniel Kirk, Megan DeFranza, Dale Martin, and I. Howard Marshall.

customs, and assumptions of their day... Some texts both reflect and challenge the cultural assumptions... by looking at what is new, rather than what is the same, sometimes we can see a trajectory towards greater liberation.[26]

Here, Hess reflects the hermeneutical idea of a redemptive ethical trajectory that has been demonstrated throughout biblical interpretation for thousands of years. As theologian Derek Flood echoes:

> ... The New Testament is not a final unchangeable eternal ethic, but rather the 'first major concrete steps' from the dominant religious and political narrative... towards a better way rooted in compassion.[27]

One biblical text where this redemptive trajectory is most clearly on display is in the Book of Acts chapter 10, where the Apostle Peter falls into a God-induced trance and is called to preach the Gospel to the unclean Gentiles for the first time. In this account, Peter sees a vision of a sheet coming out of heaven, holding a plethora of biblically 'unclean' animals. As Peter observes the sheet with confusion, he hears the voice of God speak to him three times, saying 'Rise up, kill, and eat'. Peter, being a faithful Jew and student of Scripture, argues with the voice of God, saying that he could not kill and eat these unclean animals because to do so would be a violation of Scripture. On the third time asking, the voice of God responds to Peter saying, 'Do not call unclean that which I have made

---

26 Carol Lakey Hess, *Caretakers of our Common House: Women's Development in Communities of Faith* (Nashville, Abingdon Press, 1997), p. 197–8.

27 Derek Flood, *Disarming Scripture: Cherry-picking Liberals, Violence-loving Conservatives, and Why We All Need to Learn to Read the Bible like Jesus Did* (San Francisco, Metanoia, 2014), p. 127.

clean.' With that, Peter awakens from the trance and finds the servants of Cornelius, a Roman centurion, knocking on his door, requesting that he come and speak to Cornelius and his household about the Gospel. Immediately, Peter realises that this vision was not about unclean foods but unclean people, the Gentiles. Peter reluctantly goes with the servants to Cornelius's house to preach the Gospel to them. As Peter arrives, he says to Cornelius, 'You yourselves know that it is unlawful for a Jew to associate with or to visit a Gentile; but God has shown me that I should not call anyone profane or unclean.'[28] As Peter preaches, we are told, 'while Peter was still speaking, the Holy Spirit fell upon all who heard the word.'[29] The Spirit falls upon the Gentiles – an example of the Spirit of God doing something that was previously understood to be immoral or unbiblical.

Peter's actions of entering a Gentile's home and baptising them into the Church were seen by the Apostles and elders in Jerusalem to be a grave violation of biblical law. After hearing about Peter's actions, the Council summoned Peter to meet them and they proceeded to 'criticise'[30] him for this apparent sin. Peter then recounts the entire situation, from his vision to the baptism of Cornelius' household, and concludes, saying: 'If then God gave them the same gift that he gave us when we believed in the Lord Jesus Christ, who was I that I could hinder God?'[31] When the Apostolic Council heard this, we are told, 'They praised God, saying, "Then God has given even to the Gentiles the repentance that leads to

28 Acts 10:28.
29 Acts 10:44.
30 Acts 11:2.
31 Acts 11:17.

life".'[32] Both Peter and the Council are open and willing to change their long-held theological beliefs and practices to coincide with the experiential evidence of God's Spirit working among the Gentiles. For these leaders, there is no deep biblical deliberation, but an acknowledgement that if God so desired to save the Gentiles, then the Apostles' only job was to celebrate and welcome the new thing that God was doing in their midst.

For decades, this story of the conversion of the Gentiles has been a cornerstone for inclusive theology, demonstrating both the redemptive trajectory of Scripture and the value of experience and testing the fruits. As queer theologian Patrick Cheng notes, the dissolution of clean and unclean as religious categories began to dissolve in the life and ministry of Jesus himself in the ways that he interacted with and included some of the most 'unholy' individuals in Jewish theological consciousness,[33] and this trend clearly continues in the theological approach of the earliest Apostles. Therefore, it can be logically deduced that when we observe the approach of Peter and the Apostles in regard to the authority given to continuing the revelatory work of the Holy Spirit and the role of experience, we are seeing a regular pattern of theological growth and evolution towards greater inclusivity. Cheryl Anderson writes:

> Biblical scholars are now advancing understandings of God and interpretations of the Biblical text that are different from traditional ones. Yet they are different only because they reflect the political and economic

---

32 Acts 11:18.
33 Patrick Cheng, *Radical Love: An Introduction to Queer Theology* (New York, Seabury, 2011), p. 80.

realities of women, the poor, and the foreigner and consider the impact that traditional interpretations have on these groups. Although those who uphold the traditional Christian interpretations, today's Pharisees, vilify this contextual approach, it is exactly the kind of approach that Jesus used.[34]

In our contemporary era, it seems clear that the Spirit of God continues to call humanity forward towards the higher ethical standards, and this belief is accepted by a majority of contemporary progressive Christians when they examine their theological and ethical beliefs about slavery, the treatment of women, the discipline of children, divorce, corporal punishment, and a wide array of other ethical issues in which modern Christian teaching is significantly more ethical than what is prescribed in the Scriptures. Webb goes to great lengths to demonstrate that, while the New Testament is, for instance, the final revelation of Scripture, the ethical perspectives of the New Testament have by no means been taken to their fullest realisation in the static words of Scripture itself.[35] As one explores how the abolitionists, for example, viewed the trajectory of Scripture, it becomes abundantly clear that it was their understanding of the spirit of the biblical texts, rather than the plain, literal reading of the text, that directed their theological fight to end slavery in the US and was a source of great critique from traditionalist, pro-slavery Christians.[36] The same approach must be faithfully

---

34 Anderson, *Ancient Laws and Contemporary Controversies*, p. 87.
35 William Webb, 'The Limits of a Redemptive-Movement Hermeneutic: A Focused Response to T. R. Schreiner', *Evangelical Quarterly* 75 (2003), 330.
36 Mark Noll, *The Civil War as a Theological Crisis* (Chapel Hill, University of North Carolina Press, 2015).

applied as Christians grapple with the 'clobber passages' that seem to condemn same-sex relationships.

It can be argued that, throughout the entire biblical canon, there is a trajectory that shows how the biblical authors' understanding of gender roles and sex evolved towards a more egalitarian approach. While examples of ethical regression are also present in the New Testament – for instance, when one looks at how Paul in various contexts amplifies his belief that women should be silent and submissive in church – by and large the direction of the ethical trajectories in the Bible points towards a more liberating and inclusive posture. It is in these same trajectories that the keys for full inclusion for LGBT+ people into the life of the Church can be found. As Evangelical theologian J. R. Daniel Kirk notes:

> For the same reason that we cannot claim anymore that men are better than women, for the same reason that we do not hold to a biblical view of marriage in which a man owns his wife, for the same reason that we err in excluding women from leading as they are gifted by the Spirit, the ground has been cut out from the ancient framework that excluded the notion of same-sex intercourse.[37]

The ethical trajectories of the biblical texts generally point towards more inclusive ways of seeing and being in the world. And as we will see in the next section of this book, there is much evidence to suggest that the Holy Spirit is working in and through sexual and gender minorities to bring about redemption and renewal in contemporary

---

37 J. R. Daniel Kirk, 'Trajectories Toward Gay Inclusion?', *Storied Theology* (2016), www.patheos.com/blogs/storiedtheology/2016/02/27/trajectories-toward-gay-inclusion/.

Christianity. It is this combination of biblical ethical trajectories and experience that should lead contemporary Christians on the same theological journey of Peter and the earliest Apostles. If the Spirit of God moves among LGBT+ people, who are Christians to stand in the way of the work of God? One can almost hear the Spirit speaking to the Church today saying, 'Do not call unclean that which I have made clean!'[38] once again.

In this section, we will hear stories of how LGBT+ Christians reconciled their faith and sexuality and boldly stepped into their place at the table of God's grace. Like Peter's account to the Council of Apostles, as you read these stories, I am confident that you will sense the powerful movement of God's Spirit in and through these queer lives and see the evident trajectory of the Kingdom in each story.

38 Acts 10:15.

The Bridges We Walk

Lauren Ileana Sotolongo

Lauren Ileana Sotolongo grew up in a family of Cuban immigrants, who established themselves as educators, public service professionals, and active church leaders in Southern California. With a familial passion for public service instilled at a young age, she found the intersection of her own passions within faith, social justice, and writing. She currently resides in Washington, D.C., is a proud tía to four bright-eyed revolutionaries, and can usually be found brewing coffee at a local roastery, or eating Oreos. Her favourite colours are orange and purple.

Part I

I am the third of four siblings. I was the first to 'go away' to college (living forty minutes away from my parent's house). My parents and grandparents were Cuban refugees. The foundation of our family is firm—set and dried in cement.

I am a crack in the cement.

I have been trying to reconcile two halves of my soul for years. Six months after moving to Washington, DC, the two halves met. The tension built until—after coffee with a friend—everything burst. The Physical embodiment of self spoke to the Christian expression of self. Each said the same thing. It's nice to finally meet you, but I don't think it's safe here.

What I would call 'The Spirit' spoke something different to both parts. It said: You are a whole 'one', not a disjointed 'many'. This weight isn't holy; these chains are not Mine. It is time.

I called my mom that night, and we cried. I then told the rest of my family—or they found out—slowly.

My foundation is an ocean, constantly flowing; my family's is sturdy, cemented in love. I am learning that no one can be 'home', when your own bones are hostile territory.

I am a crack in the cement. But I am learning to call the tearing of certain veils 'holy'.

I am a crack in the cement. But I think light is pushing through.

I think, even in this break, something is growing.

Part II

People got shot in a nightclub and I felt like a body on the floor. And the thing about grief is, it cannot bear any form of 'loving challenge'. Grief only knows love, or lack of love. Grief only knows an open or shut door.

After the shooting - plastered across news screens, and in the midst of our own Capital Pride in DC - I shared my grief in various social media posts.

My younger brother sent a text on a Wednesday night. It read, 'You okay?'

'I don't know', I said.

I explained briefly; it felt so personal, and heavy. People died at a nightclub. And that same night, I was out, celebrating Pride, at a nightclub. Latino people were killed. I am a Cuban American, and my parents were refugees.

I did not know how to justify my pain; only that it was intimate and deep and there.

My younger brother's response to the rocks on my chest; to the rocks in my throat; to the rocks in the thousands of miles that separated our eyes; was: 'Aight. Love you punk.'

And it was enough. My younger brother is not afraid of crossing lines; I think he is afraid of leaving someone isolated, behind lines that others won't cross. He is less worried about what his love for me means; he is more worried about not giving it.

So he gives.

And it is enough.

Part III

My father's eyelids are heavy like a velvet curtain. The autumn-leaves in his eyes, the hazelnut-coffee in his pained stare, make me feel that something inside him seems to be drowning.

My father hunts; plays poker; loves quietly; gardens consistently; breaks, builds, remodels, and fixes. He bought me my first knife at age 9. When I was younger, we used to peruse Best Buy excitedly. Home Depot, too. He would say Home Depot was 'Disneyland'; Home Depot was the place we went to fix things.

I think my father's veins are splitting, because he does not know how to fix me.

My father has a daughter who may one day bring home a woman and call her 'love'. The wooden church pews and plastic Sunday chairs we've shared for years tell my father that they can no longer hold me. He hears the echo of questions never asked, because answers spoke clearly; Romans, Sodom, Adam and Eve.

My father is a good man. He also cannot picture a wedding day for a daughter that does not include a man; one who can protect me and lead me to a good God. He cannot picture a wedding day with a woman as the fulfillment of his dreams for me; he cannot picture a wedding day, with a woman by my side; a woman who could protect and lead me to a good God.

My father and I cannot adventure through Home Depot to fix me. And I don't think my father wants this. Perhaps that makes him sad too.

He is still the sunrise to me. His eyes, autumn leaves; hazelnut coffee. He tells me stories of Cuba; of running through sugar cane fields near the railroad tracks in a run-down town. He is the sunrise to me. I want to rise with him. I wonder if - one day - he will let me.

My father's eyelids are heavy, but his eyes still shine.

My father's religion is his everything.

But - I think - so am I.

Part IV

My mother is a committed teacher. Her favourite subjects are history and forgiveness. She cherishes those lessons etched into the bones and forgotten homes of ancient people; her middle schoolers call her strict - I call her committed to the most beautiful and excellent of things.

Most weeks, I remember the lessons my mother taught me. (How to make café Cubano; entertain company; shave my legs; order pizza without fear of strangers.)

My mother is a holy rhythm I neglect. Most weeks, I dial her number like a forgotten journal entry. Her smile's soft edges (and warm eyes) are painted across my face like an echo. I carry these echoes like divine prophesy. It is the same way my brave, warrior mother used to carry me in her belly. I think, sometimes, she still tries to carry me.

Some weeks, our words share the pleasantries of afternoon tea; other weeks, they stumble into one another clumsily, like rubbing alcohol against bloody veins. There will always be things that sting, but I will choose to live in uncomfortable proximity to these things; after all, she is my veins. After all, she is this blood.

I have been entrusted to wear her smile the way I used to wear my skinned knees—proud, and rebellious, and slightly challenging the status quo.

I have been taught these things. After all, I am the daughter of a brave, warrior mother.

Most weeks, I remember that her veins are my veins, and her blood rushes through me.

Most weeks, I remember the lessons she taught me.

Part V

I babysat Nephew and Niece while Sister and Brother-In-Law visited wineries.

We rented an Airbnb in Paso Robles, California, and while the 'adults' left for the day, me and the kids watched *Little Mermaid* and sang. My nephew calls me 'Tia', and I feel there is no better title in the world.

My sister loves deeply and cries like me. We set up our walls inside our hearts differently, but it does not mean we don't understand the substance of each other's beings. She loves me.

They all do.

When I told her about my then-girlfriend, we were in her living room with a rare moment alone, together; she

93

replied, 'Lauren, you know what I think'. We usually leave things here, because we'll both cry - and have many times.

We love deeply.

They all do.

On this day, though, she returned from the winery, blustery and bright-eyed with my huggable brother-in-law. She rambled quickly about the wines; the beauty of the vineyards; the scenery and the town. She recounted it like a 7-year-old after a field trip. I recounted my trip to the park, with my tiny nephew and niece similarly, mainly because it truly felt like an attempt to summit Everest (which is what having two tiny humans in your care feels like).

She laughed at my recounting. Her eyes flashed, as if to remember something; she took a moment and added - 'Oh. And there was this cute guy working at the winery. I would've given him your number but didn't … since you're not into dudes.'

My heart stopped.

It was the closest we'd gotten to talking positively (or neutrally) about sexuality. No fight; just a simple joke. It was an open-air acknowledgment. Simple; easily missed; wildly important to me; perhaps a misunderstanding. But I do not regret misunderstanding, if I did, because this misunderstanding spelled out 'I love you'. I will take this as its meaning.

Because she loves me.

Because they all do.

Part VI

We mostly avoid eye contact when I visit. He gives a firm hug when I arrive, and a kiss on the cheek. He does the same when I leave.

I think he is acknowledging that he is losing - or has lost - something. I am his little sister. I love his two sons more than I could ever explain. His wife shines like a sunrise and cares a lot too.

It is hard to step in the fire without knowing how - or if - you'll make it out the other side. I think we're all learning the depth of this burning in my family. But Love isn't easily killed; burned at the stake; sacrificed like a body in the street, slain. Love is tougher than gold; refined and reborn like a phoenix; resurrected and remade.

My older brother follows reason like a compass - it is the arrow stuck in his heart. But Love isn't easily killed. He hugs me firmly when I come home, and he kisses me on the cheek; he does the same when I leave.

I am learning to call the simplest of things 'loving'. I am learning to hold closely, the glimpses of something more; words that none of us are ready to speak.

Let's start with a firm hug, and kiss on the cheek.

Part VII

I am a crack in the cement.
My hands are shaking, stretched until the muscles tear. My lips are cracking, my skin is cut, and blood is seeping through. But I will stop putting these red stains across manmade letters.

I will love to the bottom of a grave dug for me. I will love to the edges of heaven; I will love to the pit of my stomach and the pit of my limits. I will stop burning my

95

heart with the rams of Ancient Israel. I will remember that I claim to have found a saviour.

I will call you my Family. I will try not to burn us, in fearful sacrifice, when I get scared. I hope you will try too.

I am a crack in the cement. But I will not stop loving you.

I hope this isn't a sin too.

Unshakeable

Garrett Schlichte

Garrett Schlichte is a freelance writer working full time in higher education and living in Washington, D.C. He received his Master's degree in higher education and student affairs from the University of Connecticut where he published and presented work on the importance of empathy in peer leadership. His work can be found in the Washington Post, The Advocate, *as well as other online publications.*

Growing up in white, middle-class, Republican, Catholic South Florida, I was always the gayest person in the room. Even well before I knew I was gay, I was the gayest person in the room. In elementary school, while most boys attempted to perfect their free-throws during recess, I attempted to perfect my Ginger Spice impersonation. Other boys wanted to be with a Spice Girl, I kind of just wanted to be one. When I was in the fourth grade, freckled, bucktoothed, chubby and slightly more round than most of my classmates, with a strawberry blond bowl cut to top it all off, I was called gay for the first time. In private Catholic school we learned a lot about the Stations of the Cross, but not a whole lot about the actual teachings of Jesus. You know, love your neighbour and all that stuff.

Regardless, I got in the car later that day and asked my aunt who had picked me up, what it meant to be gay. 'Well, it just means… uhh, you're happy. Like make the yuletide gay, like happy. It means you're happy.' She seemed about as confident in her answer as I had been eating meatloaf in the cafeteria earlier that day, but given that she was the authority figure, I accepted her answer no questions asked. I spent the rest of the afternoon at my aunt's house with my cousin, holding hands, skipping and shouting, 'We're gay, we're gay, gay and gay, we're gay!' That was until my cousin's mother, a different aunt, came to pick her up and overheard us. 'Stop that! Stop it right now! I don't know who taught you that, but it's not OK. You're not gay!' We tried to explain to her that it meant happy, that we were told just a few hours before that it was a good thing, but she didn't want to listen. The discussion was over before it began. I learned then and there that 'gay' did not in fact mean happy, and was apparently, the very antithesis of the word.

Thus began the long and arduous process of repressing and ignoring what is in fact one of the most human, natural, and beautiful parts of who I am. I likely knew deep inside myself that day on the playground in the fourth grade what being gay actually meant. I probably recognised inside myself a little something that was different than most other boys I was surrounded by. However, it didn't matter. It didn't matter because it was made very clear to me that the little something that made me different, was also unwelcomed. Whether or not I recognised it as my truth didn't matter. I could know it, and did, years and years before I finally came out, but no one else could know it. If I was the only one who knew it, I was safe.

And yes, safe I was, at least in the physical sense. Flamboyant as I may have been, and trust me when I say there was no one with a limper wrist, I never incurred any physical harm in the way so many of my queer friends did. However, I was not safe from emotional and spiritual harm. When I closed off that portion of myself, and didn't allow myself to share it with anyone, I also ceased to explore any other parts of myself. In the eighth grade, I won the Religion Award for my graduating class; in high school two priests told me they saw in me someone who could be destined for the priesthood. I knew every creed, and prayer, every ritual, and major deeds of all the important saints. But I had no faith. Unable to explore who I was fully meant I couldn't engage in a spiritual life that was authentic. Partly because I was afraid that if I did, I would learn that this thing inside me that made me different, would also make me dirty.

Time went by, as it always does, and when I left home for college I soon found myself in a world of new possibilities. Days after my parents dropped me off, I came out to strangers who lived a couple of doors down from me in my residence hall. I was met with open arms, and I was thrust into a brand-new community of people who loved me for who and how I was. I was luckier than most, incredibly lucky and immensely loved. After my first year of college I came out to my parents. Again, I felt lucky and loved. Coming out is a never-ending process of self-discovery, and I am truly blessed to have the support of so many on my journey.

I began to explore a new territory of beliefs – political and social ideologies, feminism and liberalism – I rabidly consumed new philosophies and big ideas. But the door to spirituality remained closed, a frontier I decided to leave unexplored. If my private Catholic schooling had taught me one thing, it was that the realm of religion was one painted in black and white, anaesthetised and void of personality. The technicolor world of progressive thought is where I belonged, and phooey to the sterile world of faith.

Then of course, as is the way of the world, I was forced to confront my own humanity. My grandfather died and I had to, for the very first time, contemplate what I thought about the afterlife. All of a sudden, the little bubble I had blown for myself was burst, and I was for the first time confronted with the bigness of the universe.

I placated myself for some time with the notion of agnosticism, and the idea that we are all universally connected by an unnamed force, but I was not satisfied. Still too afraid to pray, I spent nights wondering if this finite existence was actually it, and was almost convinced that it was. Then, that unnamed force, which I now call God, placed into my life a boy named Zach. Several of my friends had attempted to get me to go to church with them, invitations that I rejected time and again. There was nothing in the world that would bring me willfully into a church again. Except, as I learned, an invitation from a cute Christian boy, who also happened to be gay.

Zach and I met at a birthday dinner for a mutual friend. We became friends because I was fascinated by his thoughtfulness, and he was entertained by my vulgarity. A few weeks later, we made plans to get lunch one Sunday. 'I'm free at like 1.30,' he said, 'I'm leading worship at church this Sunday. Hey, why don't you come and then we can just go from there.' It had been a while since a cute boy had invited me anywhere, so I said yes immediately.

That Sunday, I was prepared to sit in the back of the church, on my phone, and wait for it to be over. Instead, I was greeted by a wave of some of the most beautifully progressive, spiritual, wonderful humans I have ever met. I nervously hummed along to what I later came to learn was Hillsong, as an out-of-the-closet gay Christian led them in worship. I was still the gayest person in the room, but I wasn't the only gay person in the room. There was a lot I had to find out about myself before I was ready to find God, but if there is one thing I am certain of, it is that if God had any qualms with my gayness, Zach certainly wouldn't have been brought into my life. And as long as I continue to see God using gay folks to bring communities together, I will continue to be one of those gay folks with an unshakeable certainty that, in the Church Jesus told us about, we are all welcome, loved, equal, and maybe, just maybe, we have the potential to be a sixth Spice Girl.

Sure?

Claire Jones

Claire Jones grew up in the historic city of Bath, and spent much of her childhood trying to change the world with her campaigns (mostly unsuccessful) and to tell people about Jesus (again, with mixed results). She continued to aim for both by studying theology at Oxford University and then working in London as an editor for a Christian international development charity. In 2015/16 she was a member of the first cohort of the Archbishop of Canterbury's quasi-monastic community, the Community of St Anselm. Now, Claire and her partner Rose have moved up to the North East to train together for ordained ministry in the Church of England - still trying to introduce people to Jesus and change their little bit of the world.

It is a wise move, so anyone with experience will say, before you commit to spend your life in a faithful relationship with another person, to make sure you're really sure. It's not a commitment to be entered into lightly or on the spur of the moment, but wholeheartedly and responsibly, before God.

So it came to be that this modest diamond ring I'd bought with flushed cheeks and a pounding heart still sat in its box a month later, in a creaky wooden drawer next to the creaky wooden bed in an otherwise bare cell. I was on a week-long silent retreat in an ancient monastery tucked many miles out of sight of the hustle and bustle of city life. These were the silent hours in which I would listen to God harder than I'd ever listened before to make absolutely sure this was the right decision.

It wasn't my choice of person that I needed to umm and ahh over. To my own surprise, I had absolutely no doubts about her, the woman with whom I knew I wanted to share every day of the rest of my life. She had a vibrant faith, a sharp intellect, a playful wit, and she brought boundless joy to even the most mundane corners of my life. No, it was her gender that meant I needed to be sure. I'm an Evangelical through and through, and I'd been raised to believe that the only kind of lifelong intimate partnership that the Bible condoned was a man and a woman in marriage. This, and only this, could be the bedrock of society and the basis of family life – any other kind of relationship would be a rejection of God's blueprint for humanity.

Many gay Christians, especially those with an Evangelical background, have a story of troubled and even tortured teenage years, as they wrestled to come to terms with a truth about themselves that seemed to be utterly condemned by the texts they held so dear. As an apparently straight teenager, I pondered issues of sexuality and scripture from a safe distance. I searched the Scriptures for principles to follow and found faithfulness, mutuality, and not taking advantage of one another to be the values that should guide my relationships rather than heterosexuality. By the time my attraction to women became clear to me, I had studied at university level the cultural contexts, ambiguous language, and theological threads that had changed my position to an affirming one, but other people's opinions took more grappling with.

104

Church leaders and friends alike expressed their concern that I was straying from God's path. Various New Testament passages were opened for me in the hope that I'd heed the warning that homosexual offenders will not inherit the Kingdom of God. Because I am bisexual, rather than gay, some implored me to choose to do the 'right thing' – to settle down with a man and resist the temptation of women.

So when I'd fallen completely in love and I was ready to propose to this wonderful woman with whom I felt certain God had paired me, I worried that the reaction from Christians with a conservative view would make me doubt myself and doubt my relationship. Would I really always have an answer for those who condemned my love and my life? Before I put a ring on her finger, I needed to hear the go-ahead from God himself. I needed to listen to him with all the humility and obedience of heart I could muster. I needed to give him every opportunity to steer me away from this proposal if that was what he wanted. Only then would I be truly confident, whatever flaming arrows flew my way.

Silence fell. For a week, I tuned out of workplace chatter and the gossip of my friendship group. I switched off from cute family updates and romantic late-night calls. I became totally uncontactable to anyone but the Lord. For a week, I asked God to speak. I was listening. If there was anything he wanted to convict me of, anything I needed to reconsider, if I'd got it wrong on same-sex relationships – if I'd got it wrong on this relationship – then this was the time for him to tell me.

And he spoke, through prayer and Bible study and spiritual direction, gently challenging me on unexpected subjects: my fear of making big decisions, for instance. Time and again he gave me the words, 'Do not be afraid'.

With each experience of intimacy with God, each time of worship, I felt only a growing sense of peace and assurance. Still, I wondered if my failure to hear God condemn my relationship was a lack of a desire to listen. Perhaps I was shutting my ears to his warnings.

On the final night, I took out my Bible once again and opened it at Romans 1:18–32. If God wanted to tell me that homosexual relationships were immoral, surely I'd hear him through this passage – others had used it often enough to tell me exactly that.

I traced over the familiar words with my finger.

> They exchanged the truth about God for a lie… worshipped and served created things rather than the Creator… Because of this, God gave them over to shameful lusts. Even their women exchanged natural sexual relations for unnatural ones… men also abandoned natural relations with women and were inflamed with lust for one another.

I listened. Would God condemn me?

In the quiet of my heart, I heard a surprising question: 'Do you see yourself here? Does this passage describe you?' I looked again at the descriptions of people who refused to glorify and thank God, who worshipped created things, who had foolish and dark hearts. I considered the years of intimacy and relationship with God I'd had, how worshipping him had sustained me. I considered my painful awareness of my sin, how precious forgiveness and redemption through Christ was to me, and how thankfulness to God was daily on my lips.

'No,' I replied to the Lord. 'No, because you are my God. You have brought me to faith, you have taught me to worship – you have poured the light of Christ into the darkness in my heart. To see myself in that passage would be to deny all that you've done in my life. That is not me.'

My heartbeat was almost audible. Did I take that conclusion from the text by myself, or did God give it to me? It seemed so obvious when I looked at the words again. There was no way that God counted me as one who didn't know him. No way that passage could be about me. No way that it had been intended to denigrate my love for a woman.

I flipped forward to Galatians 5:19–23, another well-worn passage that had been used to frighten me in the past. I read about the contrast between the 'obvious acts of the flesh', and the fruit of the Holy Spirit.

Again, the quiet voice came. God whispered, 'Where do you see your relationship? Which list describes its fruit?' I compared the two options – impurity, debauchery, hatred, rage, selfishness, envy, and drunkenness? Those things had certainly featured in my life before this relationship. In seasons of singleness I'd been prone to self-centredness, and there had been times when my socialising could well have been described as less than pure.

But those things were not the fruit I saw now. Not with her. Rather, the qualities on the other list, the description of the Spirit's fruit, these were what rung true. Love – yes. I saw that in my life now. Joy and peace – absolutely. Being with her brought out the best in me, made me more loving, more patient, more kind, and more faithful than I'd ever been before. I felt more fully alive, more fully myself than I'd known I could be. Wrapped up in her love, I got to benefit from the beautiful fruit in her too.

Where my life had been sometimes restless, often lacking in self-control, and filled with more frustration than joy, now I was flourishing. No one who knew the two of us well could deny that God's Spirit was at work in our relationship. The fruit in our lives was tangible.

God seemed to be resting his case. 'Don't be afraid,' he'd been saying all week. 'Don't be afraid of those who use the Bible as a weapon. Don't be afraid; I am for you. Don't be afraid; I am in your love.'

Peace filled me and settled with me. That night, I went to sleep content that I would, the next day, ask the woman I loved to spend the rest of her life with me. Now I knew for sure that there would be rejoicing in heaven at the moment she said yes.

Oh Wait, That's Me

Matthias Roberts

Matthias Roberts is a writer, speaker and host of Queerology: A Podcast on Belief and Being. *He holds an MA in Theology and Culture and is currently finishing his second master's in Counseling Psychology at the Seattle School of Theology and Psychology. Matthias blogs at www.matthiasroberts.com*

There are times I forget I'm gay.

It's not hard to do. I'll be walking the rainy streets of downtown Seattle with my new bag slung over my shoulder and the fashionable raincoat that was oh-so-difficult to find and I'll feel normal. People will smile at me. I'll smile back, or at least, I think I'm smiling. Until my boss tells me later, 'I saw you walking on 1st today! You look so angry when you walk around.' I thought I was being friendly, but then, he probably didn't see me when I waved at that dog.

I've been waiting for a long time to feel normal. In the world from which I came, normal had very strict boundaries. We called it 'biblical'. Manhood, womanhood, marriage, whatever – in order to be normal, it had to fit within a certain framework. I didn't. If you look through my mom's photo albums from my childhood, you'll find me wearing princess dresses and full makeup posing with my sisters. No wonder my aunt wasn't surprised when I sent her that email telling her about my 'same-sex attractions'. I'm still a little bit annoyed it wasn't a shock. I thought I had been hiding it so well behind that awful orange community theatre curtain.

I grew up in the Midwest. More middle than west. Smack dab in the centre of a cornfield in Iowa, give or take some years in Wisconsin. My family was deep within the clutches of conservative Christianity. Normal wasn't an option for me. It was only something to observe and attempt to mimic. What do the other boys like? Oh, okay, I like that too now. 'Hilary Duff? I adore her!' Wait, not like that. Apparently, the guys in my Boy Scout troop didn't dream of being Lizzie McGuire on stage singing 'What Dreams Are Made Of' from the classic movie when she visits Rome.

Normal meant squeezing and pushing and diminishing every single part of me that was different until my outside shell fit and my inside didn't exist. I still get told every once in a while: 'I'd have no idea you were gay unless I had asked!' That puzzles me. They must at least wonder? I don't think people generally go around enquiring about sexual orientation. But, I'll take it. I still get a strange sense of pride from passing as straight, even if only somewhat. You can probably call that internalised homophobia. It's something I'm still trying to get over. And no, it's not a fear sent from God to show me the error of my ways. Want to talk about demons? Let's talk about a culture that teaches people who are different to hate themselves.

In order to fit in, I had to learn the language and talk about girls as if I were really into them. I had to learn how to smile and push away any and all attraction that might appear when a really hot guy in youth group started talking to me. I'd usually just avoid him; he'd probably call me a girl anyway. Being attracted to men was always on my mind. Hypervigilance. No one could ever find out.

Intense hatred and fear directed at my little body that had no idea what was going on.

I had no idea what was going on.

*

It amazes me that I can now walk through the Seattle mist and not give my being a second thought. I'll breathe in the salty air from Puget Sound, grab some flowers from the market, and arrange them on the IKEA table in the tiny downtown studio apartment I rent. It's a life I've dreamed of and here it is, happening now.

A few months ago, I went on my first date, ever. He didn't know that. My therapist tells me I have a preoccupied attachment style which means I have a hard time believing I'm worthy of love. That feels true to me. There are times I wonder why I can't find goodness within myself, especially in regard to someday actually being in a relationship with a man. But, then I remember that the first 22 years of my life were filled with messages that told me explicitly I couldn't love. No wonder I have work to do.

That first date was magical, I had to keep reminding myself it was actually happening, it felt so natural and normal. Fluid. Like the water that runs down my umbrella when I decide I just cannot stand being a pretentious Seattleite who 'doesn't use an umbrella'. We went to the restaurant where I work. I had a gift card left over from last Christmas. It spent ten months sitting on my desk collecting dust because I kept projecting a hope that I'd get to use it on somebody special. Two hours into the meal, I spotted Chef spying on us from across the room divider – he didn't think I noticed, 'you two were just so lost in each other's eyes'.

That makes me roll the blue eyes I'm just learning to see as an attractive feature of my face. When a person spends years hearing he is unworthy of romantic relationship, the self-loathing doesn't just magically disappear. I don't know if I was lost in his eyes. I thought that was something that only happens in the movies. But the idea of seeing myself so wrapped up in another's eyes makes my stomach jump with giddiness. His eyes are really beautiful. Is this what high-schoolers feel like when they fall in love for the first time?

Love is a strong word. There wasn't a second date. That felt mature and healthy to my adult-brain. But, a part of me still feels stuck in adolescence. Why couldn't we have just called ourselves boyfriends immediately? He didn't want a relationship. When I stopped and wrote a list about what I actually wanted, I'm not sure I wanted to be in a relationship either. There's a disconnect. I feel like there are some things I should have learned years ago and I have no idea what they are.

*

Sometimes, I'll overhear a conversation in the coffee shop I frequent about LGBT+ people and how they're trying to ruin the world. It's not a secret that this shop had loose ties to a certain church dynasty that came crumbling down a couple of years ago. I go anyway. I really like their coffee. I also really like the chicken nuggets at that one place we were supposed to boycott too. Whoops.

My ears will perk up, like they always do when I hear anything resembling a conversation around sexuality. *Fascinating*, I'll think, *these people are just so different than me. Oh wait*, I'll pause, *that's me*. I'm the person they're referring to. The one who's trying to ruin the world one mocha at a time. I forget about that.

There are so many who are back where I used to be, never able to forget, always remembering they're different. It doesn't matter how many welcome mats a church puts out, or how many times 'safe' is used in a conversation. If one has to hide who they are in order to fit in, none of those sentiments make any difference. They just rip apart even more. I'm trying to find all the pieces and put myself back together.

I burst into tears the morning after the date. The sobbing surprised me. I had just put on one of my favourite worship albums and as I went into the bathroom to pee the tears started escaping. I barely even had time to grab my already wet towel from my earlier shower. I moved to my bed, clutched my pillow, and wrenched for a half hour. Deep soul-level tears. An emotional escape I didn't even realise I needed. Yet, that in itself is something I'm learning to celebrate. I spent 11 years of my life unable to cry. When you cut off one part of yourself, you often cut off many others as well.

I don't even know why I was crying. I texted my friend who is also a crier and she just said 'welcome to the club'. I think my therapist would call this congruence. I'm not sure if I like it – bursting into tears while peeing is not an experience I want to become commonplace in my life. The tears themselves though – the saltiness, the way they soak into my pillow and make it all wet – they remind me of the salty wetness of this city that is helping me make all things new.

There's a verse I was reading the other day: '… be transformed by the renewing of your mind.' I never imagined renewal to consist of salt and dampness and pillow clutching. Or staring a boy in the eyes over steak for three hours. And yet, I feel the newness, the freshness. I feel. And I'm not faking it. There is room to be unhappy, there is room to be angry, I don't have to pretend. I can walk down the street without a smile on my face. I can wave at a dog and feel a burst of happiness.

There are times I see myself as if I were watching a movie. There's that boy walking down 1st with his beautiful raincoat and brand-new bag. I'm not sure he's the main character, but he's learning to be. It's the kind of movie where boys do get lost in each other's eyes and the characters, all of them, live happily ever after in the glorious messiness of their lives. There's that boy, he's so... gay.

Oh wait. That's me.

The Amazing, Invisible Bisexual Christian

Kathleen Jowitt

Kathleen Jowitt is an author and trade union officer. Her first novel, Speak Its Name, *explores the interplay between Christianity and sexual identity in the context of student life and politics. She lives in Cambridge, UK, and identifies as bisexual and Anglican.*

When I came out the first time, I was engaged.

No. When I came out the first time, it was as simple a thing as a note in my diary, so matter-of-fact and low-key that I missed it when I was writing the first draft of this essay.

When I came out the second time, I was engaged. Sometimes I say, only half-joking, that it was because I was engaged that I came out: the marriage preparation course made me take a long, hard look at myself, and acknowledge some significant parts that I had previously been ignoring. An own goal for the Church of England? From this distance, I don't care. The only thing that matters now is that I came out to my fiancé. I wanted to be sure, before we took this step, that we both knew who I was.

Perhaps it isn't so unusual. Of all the L, G, B or T Christians I know, the huge majority are bisexual women. The majority of those are in opposite-sex relationships.

One of them got married a couple of years ago. It was a church wedding and the priest wore a rainbow stole. Perhaps it's easier knowing that one does, after all, have the option of passing as straight if it gets as bad as all that. I don't know. In my experience passing as straight is almost as tiring as repeatedly coming out.

I am a bisexual Anglican. I know bisexual Catholics, Methodists, Quakers. There are lots of us. We are not obvious, but we are there. I thank God – quite literally – that I was not brought up a biblical literalist, believing that I had to follow every single verse of the Bible to the letter, particularly the ones in Leviticus and Romans. It saved me a huge amount of angst. I was quite happy being Christian and bisexual. I could see no conflict between these two parts of my identity, so long as I was living a life of sexual and emotional integrity. And I was - except for the fact that I knew that people were assuming that I was straight.

The next time I came out I was married and very aware of my privilege. The question of same-sex marriage was dominating the news then and I was passionately – if silently – in favour of it. I had been lucky enough to fall in love with somebody I could legally marry. I knew how easily it could have gone the other way.

My church held an evening debate to discuss what the parish's position should be. I didn't speak. I didn't need to. It was the sort of church where intelligent people put across coherent, convincing arguments for same-sex marriage as a matter of course. I didn't feel that I had anything to add. At the same time, I would have liked to have spoken because I would have liked to be out. I didn't really regret it, though, until I was walking home with a couple of other people who'd been there.

'I don't know,' one said. 'I'm not sure it's the same thing. Is it really what these people want?'

I should have said - I wanted to say, 'But it's not "these people". It's me. It could very easily be me,' but I couldn't. I was very invisible then.

I went to see the rector soon after that. I did that every couple of years. He was very good at helping me unravel what was going on in my mind. This time, I had one thing on my mind.

'I feel that I ought to come out,' I said.

He pounced on that. It turned out that the two most important words in that sentence were not 'come out' but 'ought to'. I felt that I ought to come out because otherwise I was contributing to bisexual invisibility. I'd got so hung up on my identity as a walking, talking political campaign that I'd completely lost sight of what I needed to do as one individual bisexual.

We did a lot of untangling and separated the guilt around being invisible, the fear around being out, and the vital point that I'd somehow managed to miss – that I didn't actually have to be out if I wasn't ready to be out, that other people were going to think things about me that weren't necessarily true, and that it wasn't my job to police their thoughts. That I was where I needed to be.

I didn't come out again for quite a while after that, but I stopped feeling so awful about it.

Another couple of years on, I'd moved job and house and region. I was a new face and rather to my surprise, I was invited to join a prayer group. Apart from anything else, I was impressed at their having pegged me as a Christian without any physical giveaway. I hadn't worn a cross or spoken of belonging to any church. Having entered a new phase of my life with joyous expectation and the intention of saying 'yes' to everything I could reasonably say 'yes' to, I joined. I wanted to give it a try, no matter how much I suspected it wasn't going to be my style.

It wasn't my style. That much became obvious in the space of my first meeting. Still, style isn't everything and this was an enthusiastic and welcoming group. The prayer was heartfelt and the Spirit was among us. There were a few prayers that made me a little uncomfortable, but on the whole I was able to take the spirit rather than the letter and say 'Amen'. So it went on for perhaps four or five meetings until I hit my personal barrier.

The petitioner asked the group (all women) to pray for 'our men'. 'Our men' were not, she felt, acting as God intended, not fulfilling their ordained role as head of the woman. That got my hackles up, but it was only the start of it. She went on, 'they're falling in love with each other...'.

It's not that she trailed off there. I just can't remember anything else of what she said. I can't remember how the leader turned that into a prayer. I can't remember any more words. I only remember the white heat of anger rising within me. I remember pelting away from that room, swirling up the stairs like lava from an erupting volcano.

I am still proud of the email that I wrote to resign from that group:

> Dear friends,
>
> I am emailing to let you know that I will not be attending the prayer group from now on.
>
> I felt that I could not say a sincere 'Amen' to some of yesterday's prayers. We spoke of how God cannot be disillusioned in us, because God has no illusions about us. I am bisexual and I cannot pray for this to change, either for myself or for others, because I know God's peace in

accepting this identity. God sees to the heart of me and loves the creature that He made.

I will continue to pray for you all, but it is best for all our sakes that I do this alone.

In Christ,

Kathleen

When I wrote that I considered glossing over my own sexual identity. I had heard enough to give me plenty of reasons for never going back, but it was a now or never moment. If I didn't tell these people, I might never tell anyone again. I wanted them to know that there were other ways to be, that it was possible to be Christian, bisexual, and at peace with my identity.

I have not gone back. This is not quite the end of the story. A few weeks later, the woman who had first said those things sent me a link to a broadcast by an American Evangelical preacher. I did not listen to it. A friend listened to it for me, and confirmed that I had been right to trust my instincts, and avoid having to listen to things like 'the opposite of homosexual is not heterosexual, the opposite of homosexual is holy'. I emailed back, explaining that it was offensive and hurtful, and asking her not to send me anything like that again. I tried to receive what I had been given in a spirit of gratefulness for her concern and to reject the offensive, hurtful wrapping paper with love and grace. It is about as difficult as it sounds.

Now I've found a church and sometimes I wear a cross that hangs from a rainbow bead. I'm letting people draw their own conclusions.

Where next? I want to be permanently, irrevocably out at church, to stop having to tell people. I want to continue working within the Church of England to make it more inclusive and welcoming. I would like to find or set up a network of bisexual Christians, a place where we can just be ourselves.

I want to trust that, even on the days when I'm too tired to argue, when I'm too hurt to forgive, when I'm too scared to be out, my being there at all is helping, somehow.

On Being a Professional Queer Christian

Neil Cazares-Thomas

The Reverend Dr Neil G. Cazares-Thomas has been the Senior Pastor of Cathedral of Hope of Dallas, a 4500-member congregation, since 3 June 2015. He attended St John's Theological College (Church of England), La Sainte Union (Roman Catholic), and King Alfred's College, and graduated with a BA (MDiv – US equivalent). In 2002 he enrolled in the Doctoral programme at San Francisco Theological Seminary (Presbyterian), graduated as a Doctor of Ministry in October 2008, and has since been granted Privilege of Call in the United Church of Christ. Dr Cazares-Thomas is a contributing author of three books, Daring to Speak Love's Name *(Penguin Books, 1993),* From Queer to Eternity *(Cassell, 1997), and* The Queer Bible Commentary *(SCM Press, 2006), and has also been featured in a number of journals relating to queer theology and ministry to the LGBT+ community.*

I was raised in England in the Church of Jesus Christ of Latter-day Saints, otherwise known as the Mormon tradition. My mother and father converted to Mormonism before I was born. They had previously been, at least nominally, Anglican (Church of England). I have said, many times before, that anything was more exciting than the

Church of England. The Mormon Church presented something that was lacking in their spiritual life.

I am one of seven children, my identical twin brother and I being the youngest. I have five brothers and one sister, so we fit into the Mormon family identity very well. By the time I was two years old, my mother and father had divorced but we remained members of the Church.

My early memories of the Church are very good. Unlike many of my contemporaries raised in other parts of the world, especially those in Evangelical and fundamentalist churches in the US, I survived very well.

By the time I was about nine years old, my mother had met someone she wanted to marry. While planning to do so, she visited with the bishop at our local Mormon Church to discuss being married there. The bishop informed her that marriage was permitted only for members of the Church. Because my soon-to-be stepfather was not a Mormon, this was not allowed. After many years of faithful church attendance, tithing, and involvement at many levels, she was rejected and told that her marriage was not good enough. These were words I would later hear about myself. The treatment of my mother by the Church taught me a valuable lesson.

We left the Mormon Church and, like so many others, became a family that was not affiliated with any church or spiritual community. The Church had given up on my mother and we had given up on the Church. I learned that the Church was an institution made up of human beings with human-made rules and regulations. No matter how hard I tried, I could not find anything in the text I held sacred that justified this treatment of our family by the Church.

Fast-forwarding a few years, I was beginning to understand that my sexual orientation was not quite the same as that of my siblings. I watched my brothers and sister date people of the opposite gender while I felt attracted to those of my gender.

I had heard only negative things about homosexuality in England from more evangelical churches. As I had left the Mormon Church at an early age, I had not heard anything directly. Therefore, I suffered very little from toxic theology. That all changed when I came out and discovered the world of religiosity.

Fortunately, coming out at fifteen was a good experience, though I will spare you the details. To a great degree, members of my family were very supportive. I eventually found myself at the local Metropolitan Community Church (MCC) in my hometown of Bournemouth, England. It was a small church filled with people committed to the life of Jesus and making Jesus real in their life.

My mother has always told me there was something different about me. She was not referring to my sexuality but to my spirituality. Even after leaving the Mormon Church, I would long to be in worship. On Sundays, I would take myself off to any local church: Baptist (not to be confused with Southern Baptist), Methodist, Church of England. I would try them all and enjoy the music, fellowship, and preaching. I had always felt a call on my life to the professional ministry. Now a member of MCC, I entered seminary in England at eighteen. I graduated at twenty-two and was ordained at twenty-three. I have served the Church for 27 years thus far.

Seminary was where I first encountered toxic theology. I entered seminary as an out gay man and never tried to hide my sexual orientation. Studying among other seminarians from many different denominations demonstrated to me just how toxic theology can be. A place of liberation often becomes the most controlling place on earth. Ironic, really – and hypocritical.

During the day, I would be told that I was an abomination. At night, those same men would want to 'come and talk' to me about their own homosexual feelings; sad and frightening.

I have since pastored two churches and recently began pastoring my third. I served the first, in Bournemouth, England, for 12 years. I served the second, Founders Metropolitan Community Church in Los Angeles, California, for nearly 14 years. They were both great experiences. I had the opportunity and distinct honour to work with many LGBT+ people harmed by toxic theology and religion. I have watched their lives transform on a journey to wholeness as they came to a progressive understanding of God, scripture, and themselves.

Today, I am the Senior Pastor at Cathedral of Hope United Church of Christ, a 4000-member congregation in Dallas, Texas. CoH is a vibrant, inclusive and progressive congregation on a mission to reclaim Christianity as a faith of extravagant grace, radical inclusion and relentless compassion. Founded in 1972, it has a long history of inclusion to LGBT+ people and, while there are many 'open and affirming' churches today, CoH sees itself as, 'Open and Celebrating'. It seeks to build a bigger table with an invitation to build an authentic, hope-filled, spiritual community.

I have married, buried, and baptised. I have been a part of many conversations with more conservative Christians and leaders who were open to understanding and journeying with me towards making room at the table for more of God's people, including God's LGBT+ people. I have watched the Holy Spirit inspire an ethic of radical inclusion. I have had the great privilege of working with that same Holy Spirit in literally saving the lives of people who, because of religious baggage and toxic theology, were contemplating suicide. And, I have grieved the loss of many who chose that path when the burden was too great, when they sincerely believed that the God of Love did not, and could not, love them.

This damage and abuse of Christianity by some is the sin of the Church. That sin is not only committed against those who are LGBT+. Besides homophobia, biphobia, and transphobia, it is evident in the sins of racism, sexism, misogyny, and many other labels used by culture and the Church to demonise 'other'. The people Christ came to love are the ones the Church is rejecting. 'The stone the builders rejected has become the cornerstone.' (Psalm 118:22) It is because of this that I continue the work that I do.

In 2008, I graduated with my Doctor of Ministry from San Francisco Theological Seminary, a Presbyterian school in Marin County, California. In June 2016, I was elected Senior Pastor of Cathedral of Hope United Church of Christ, a 4500-member congregation in Dallas, Texas. It boldly claims as its mission: 'Reclaim Christianity as a faith of extravagant grace, radical inclusion, and relentless compassion.'

Again and again, I return to the experience of my mother all those years ago. She was told her marriage was not good enough, and contrary to God's word. I remind myself that there is a big difference between 'churchianity' and 'Christianity'. I hold to my deep faith in Jesus, who commands us to 'love God, love others, love self'. I call myself back to the simple knowledge that God is love, and instructs us to 'love one another as I have loved you'. These simple truths are truth for us all, regardless of age, colour, gender, gender identity, class, physical ability, education, health status, etc. This is the work of the Spirit. This is the work of the followers of Jesus.

Today, I am bold enough, confident enough, and loved enough to know that Christianity is a lifestyle choice you put on every day. I can reject the dogma of any religion established to impose and maintain control. I can live by the values of Jesus that always lead to freedom, authenticity, light, and love.

Hallelujah!

All of Me

Kevin Garcia

Kevin Garcia is a writer, blogger, podcaster, and creative who is making his way into full-time content creation, making videos, blogs, and podcasts that reflect the diverse LGBT+ experience. Since graduating from Christopher Newport University in 2013 with a Bachelor of Music, he's been everything from a voice coach, to a missionary, to a corporate office worker, to a barista, and everything in between. Since coming out as a gay Christian in autumn 2015, he's connected with thousands of people through his blog and podcast, hoping to empower people to live a fearlessly authentic life while helping to create safer spaces in Christian communities. He blogs regularly at theKevinGarcia.com, hosts a podcast called A Tiny Revolution, and leads worship with his small group. When he's not trying to dismantle the white, cis, heterosexist capitalist patriarchy, you can find him drinking way too much coffee, making tacos, or getting into some form of tomfoolery with his incredible community in Atlanta, Georgia.

I had a friend who asked me why I was still a Christian. Why do I still worship at one of those sort-of-progressive Evangelical churches? Why do I still decide to work and do life in a space that doesn't honour the fullness of who I am? 'Why don't you just become Episcopalian? They've been cool with the gays for a while.'

127

Trust me, I've asked myself the same question many a time. In fact, I ask it every Sunday when I go to the 7.00 p.m. worship service. Some Sundays, I must confess, my answer is a big fat 'I don't freaking know' accompanied by a groan of self-reproach and my hands thrown in the air.

It would honestly be so much simpler to be a part of a tradition that allowed me to be myself. It would be easier to work in my calling without fighting to defend my dignity and my calling, as a baptised person, to be a minister to my community. I wonder what it would be like to not only bring my full self into a space, but to have my full self celebrated by my community.

That's the problem with so many churches these days. They use big buzzwords like authenticity, transparency, or other fluffy notions that circle that same idea of bringing your full self. Granted, it's better than what I grew up with, which was completely about keeping up appearances, celebrating the blessed life in spite of extreme pain, staying in line, and never asking questions.

What so many churches don't realise is they don't actually believe their own rhetoric. When someone like a white, straight, cisgender, male pastor says, 'Come as you are,' there is a silent question whispered in the hearts of so many hurting and different people, especially LGBT+ folks:

'Do you really mean that?'

We have seen what happens with those the Church doesn't want or doesn't like. It usually looks painful, ranging from excommunication to being burned at the stake. We know countless stories of those who lost everything because they simply told the truth about who they were.

And so, rather than suffer that pain, we either lie about who we are, or we run away from our communities. We hope to forego the pain of rejection by rejecting them first. We separate our lives into quadrants that never touch or intersect. We have our work lives, spiritual lives, church lives, social lives, sex lives, and so on. We separate our good nature from our bad nature. We ascribe everything we don't like about ourselves to our 'flesh' and try to place it on the altar, hoping it simply burns up and goes away.

What we do when we separate our lives in this way is separate our heart. We separate the singular, integrated being that God lovingly crafted. We compartmentalise our pain, opting for only joy, not knowing that they depend on each other. How can we know the heights of ecstasy if we never know the depths of sorrow? We push away any negative attributes about ourselves, be it jealousy or anger. We say those things aren't a part of us, rather than owning our sins and being able to truly repent.

The same goes with our sexuality. When we divorce ourselves of our natural sexual expression – gay, or straight, or otherwise – we are deeply affected. By attaching sexuality to our sin nature, our flesh, a thing we want to separate ourselves from, we learn to abhor it. We learn to hate it. We learn that we must kill it.

What is terrifying about this mindset is the attitude of outright violence towards ourselves. It can manifest itself in addiction to numb our pain or attempt to cope with our personal grief. It can also present in mental illness, actual physical ailments, self-harm, and even suicide.

...

I made a woman fall in love with me once. I knew all the right things to say, all the right things I should do as a boyfriend and future spouse. I knew about my role as the leader in the relationship. I knew how to honour her and God by abstaining from sex until our marriage night. I knew that this was the path God had for me. I just knew it.

I was in my mid twenties at the time. After over a decade in ex-gay therapy, I had this frightening realisation that my attraction to men would probably never go away. Despite that, I rationalised that just because I was attracted to men didn't mean that I couldn't marry a woman. That was, after all, God's best.

I had gotten to the point where I could have made that happen. I had done all the right things, taken all the right steps, and really meditated on what it was to love someone for all of who they were with all of who you were. That was when I realised I couldn't do any of that, and that everything I did was for the wrong reasons.

I was with her because I needed to be assured of God's love for me, not to assure her of my love for her. I was chasing after marriage because that would be the sign of my faithfulness to God, not my undying devotion to her.

I could never love her fully because I didn't even like myself a little. I could never love her fully because I simply couldn't. I wasn't created that way. I wasn't struggling with my sexuality. I was gay. And it was beyond obvious that nothing, not even God, was going to change that.

Our break-up sent me into a tailspin. I started smoking again. Then, I moved towards entertaining the idea of driving my car into a lake and slowly slipping into nothingness as breath left my lungs. I was beyond disgusted with myself and distraught that I couldn't please God because I couldn't get my flesh under my dominion.

What you might be interested to know is that, through all this, I had read a ton of progressive and affirming theology. I understood the arguments for LGBT+ inclusion in the Church. I even believed for a while, perhaps God gives some people the freedom to do things, but not others; as if God saved the true suffering for the strongest servants. I wanted it all to be true, but it couldn't be true for me. I was too unlovely, had done too much wrong, told too many lies, and hurt too many people for my life to ever be redeemed.

The thing about separating our hearts is, in the separation, darkness tends to creep in. The worst words and most horrible feelings and fears take root in the spaces between. These roots trap our hearts, causing them to turn hard toward ourselves. We are unable to see things for what they are, and unable to receive anything new from God.

But, it is in that moment, when all hope is lost and the world is frozen in fear, that God comes in with a river of grace to wash away everything we thought we knew and replace it with a peace to be okay with never fully comprehending.

...

Shortly after our break-up, I attended a conference. Not knowing what to expect, but desperately needing some answers, I walked into a room full of strangers. I sat a few rows back and just prayed that God would speak. I wanted either the confirmation that I needed to commit to celibacy, or that maybe...

Maybe something else was possible. Maybe there was a different way to live because, at that point, I didn't know how I could remain where I was.

When the worship music started, I lifted my hands, like I always do, and I just waited. Something happened next that I can't quite describe. My body felt heavy, gently giving way to this waterfall of light and electricity and gold just bearing down on me. It felt warm and bright and full. It engulfed me and I began to cry silent tears, in awe of the Presence that had come to me. It was like nothing I ever felt before.

131

In an instant, I was filled with a zeal to live like never before, where before I had been so desperate to die. I was confident in the direction my life was headed because I knew it was going to be towards God.

And yes, that does sound crazy. But, it's no crazier than when my body was healed instantly because we prayed for it. It's no crazier than the spot-on, prophetic words I have received over the years. And, it's certainly no crazier than the confession that I believe a rabbi over 2000 years ago, who was executed by the state, rose from the dead and was the literal son of God.

In that moment, there was this sense of wholeness I'd never felt before, a peace that said this is what I was created for. I came into a space with my full self and allowed myself to be celebrated in the fullness of who I was. I allowed all the aspects of my life that I had separated out to become one again, reuniting me with my Divine design, and reconnecting me with my Divine Union with the Spirit.

Since then, I have never been more sure of my calling as a son of God. I've never been more compelled by the teachings of Jesus to do good in the world, to strive to walk humbly, live mercifully, or love even those who hurt me. I have never been more connected to the Holy Spirit and the supernatural work done around me, in me, and for me. I feel a fullness and overflowing of God in ways that wouldn't have been possible before, when I was living in shame of who I was created to be.

...

So, why am I still a Christian? Why do I still worship at one of those sort-of-progressive Evangelical churches? Why do I still decide to work and do life in a space that doesn't honour the fullness of who I am?

I'm still a Christian because I've seen too much. I've experienced too much of the fullness of God to just chalk it up to mere coincidence or emotional overstimulation. I've had these weird, mystical and mysterious things happen to me that are beyond explanation. Sometimes we call things beyond explanation miracles.

I stay in Evangelical circles because it is the Evangelical Church which introduced me to a Jesus who loved the outsider and championed those who were hurting. For better or for worse, they are my family. And, I want my family to experience the fully integrated life, the abundant life Jesus talked about.

I do life in a space that doesn't honour the fullness of who I am because I don't need another person to tell me I am worthy or welcome. I understand that Jesus welcomes me. The body is for me. The blood is for me. No one gets to tell me that this is untrue. I stay because I see the humanity in those who can't or won't see it in me, and I am called to restore sight to the blind.

All of me is welcome in God's presence: even the parts I don't like; even the parts I wish didn't exist; even my anger, jealousy, and fear. It all belongs and is all needed to fully be human. My wholeness is my gift to the world. I come as I am, fully and totally myself, as a prophetic gesture of where we are headed. There will be a day when churches everywhere say, 'Come as you are,' and mean it completely, for everyone, without exception.

What a day that will be.

And so it Goes

Paula Williams

The Revd Dr Paula Williams was the CEO of a large church planting organisation, a megachurch preaching pastor, a magazine editor, and a seminary instructor. All ended when she transitioned from Paul to Paula. After 35 years in New York, Paula moved to Denver, Colorado, where she currently serves as a pastoral counsellor, coach, and church consultant. She works with OPEN, a network of progressive Evangelicals, coaches with the Center for Progressive Renewal, and directs the church planting team at Highlands Church in Denver. Paula also serves on the board of the Gay Christian Network and is a blogger for the Huffington Post. *For more information visit paulastonewilliams.com.*

I was never sure I believed in God. Given that I was a pastor and all, this was a problem. I had read Francis Schaeffer's *He Is There and He Is Not Silent,* which brought me closer to the holy grail of belief, but not close enough. Schaeffer worked for me because I was a thinker, not a feeler. Feelings, I had learned early, were not safe.

I was probably three or four when I knew I was a girl, yet no one treated me like the girl I knew myself to be. In the way children learn so well, I stuffed my feelings. My body appeared to be the body of a boy. Therefore I was a boy, feelings be damned. If I could not feel my way to wholeness, I would think my way there. Hence the problem with God. Try as you might, you cannot think yourself into belief in God.

My father was a pastor, a kind man from a theologically conservative background, whose life betrayed his theology. Dad rejected no one. I took notice. My mother was, in every way, more conservative. She did not see the world as safe, and the God who created it was no exception. God was not partial to anyone's feelings, and apparently didn't have any himself, since he had passively watched his own son die and all.

Believing in God meant making sense of an Ultimate Disciplinarian who apparently did not really care if I made it to heaven. Through Bible college and seminary I fashioned some understanding of God that allowed me to enter ministry with a modicum of integrity. I never appreciated Josh McDowell's *Evidence that Demands a Verdict*, finding more convincing arguments from Francis Collins, John Polkinghorne, and Owen Gingerich. Still, there was this gnawing fear my apologetic had been created out of construction paper and did not have a prayer of withstanding a tree-bending storm.

The storm arrived when I was watching my favourite television show of all time, *Lost*. Damon Lindelof and Carlton Cuse were the showrunners. The series probed the liminal space between faith and reason, the writers playing word games with history. John Locke was not Lockean, but a man engrossed in mystery. Jack, the show's main protagonist and son of a man named Christian, was very Lockean. Jack was a Western physician, committed to science, not dwelling in the realm of mystery and faith. However, in the sixth and final season Jack came to realise that Jacob (God) was real, and he had been called to sacrifice his life for the sake of his friends.

Section 2: Reconciliation

The night that show aired I was alone in my Colorado home. When Jack had his epiphany I began to wail. I wept as I had never wept before. I screamed and railed at God, 'Who do you think you are to have made me this way and called me to this? I'm going to lose everything. Don't you know what this is going to do to my family?' The only sound was silence, but there was no doubt in my heart, I had been called to be Paula.

I was well known in the Evangelical world, the CEO of a four-million-dollar ministry, the editor-at-large and weekly columnist of a venerable Christian magazine, a megachurch preaching pastor, and a seminary instructor. In my Evangelical bubble, this was not going to go well.

When I came out on my blog (paulastonewilliams.com) there were over 65,000 page views, and most of those people were angry. I lost all of my jobs and thousands of Christian friends. I assumed my time in the Church was over. It would be reasonable to assume my faith departed with my employment, but tenuous as my faith had always been, it did not abandon me. To the contrary, it transformed me.

A 2014 study[1] by Sara Burke and Julie Bakker, two psychologists in the Netherlands, looked at the MRI results of 80 pre-hormone-treated transgender individuals. Among other findings, the scientists discovered that the participants responded to an odorous steroid in the area of the hypothalamus consistent with the brains of the gender with which they identified. That was before hormone therapy. As I discovered on oestrogen and anti-androgens, hormone treatment changes the brain significantly.

1   Burke, Sarah M. et al. 'Hypothalamic Response to the Chemo-Signal Androstadienone in Gender Dysphoric Children and Adolescents.' *Frontiers in Endocrinology* 5 (2014): 60. *PMC*. Web. 29 Aug. 2017.

Nowhere were the changes any more significant than in the realm of spirituality and sexuality.

Sexuality and spirituality are closely intertwined. The most common phrase repeated at sexual climax is, 'Oh God!' I believe there is a reason. With oestrogen and anti-androgens, my sexuality and spirituality both changed massively. Since it deserves an entire chapter, or better yet, an entire book, I will save the changes in how I now experience sexuality for some later time. For now, I will focus on the spiritual changes.

I have a friend who is a camera operator in the feature film business. For years he insisted I watch *Babette's Feast*. I finally rented the film and found it did not do much for me. A few years after I became Paula I watched the film again. Oh my! The change was not in the movie. The change was in me. Paul found spirituality in proper exegesis and good hermeneutics. Paula finds spirituality in a meal with friends, in the wisdom of mothers, and in the space between human relationships. I still appreciate good exegesis and a proper hermeneutic, but spirituality is so much more.

One of my closest friends is Jen Jepsen, a woman who once knew Paul and was willing to go through the discomfort of getting to know Paula. A couple of years ago Jen began attending Highlands Church in Denver. A few months later I joined her there.

On my first Sunday, I could not bring myself to go forward for communion. Jen brought the moistened bread back in her cupped hands, precious as a gift from the Magi. As I ate the bread, I knew for the second time I had been called by God. This time I was called back to the Church. Within three months I was preaching at Highlands.

I do not know what to make of my newfound holistic faith. It is not important that I understand it. It is important that I experience the love of the Father, the heart-wrenching solidarity in the suffering of the Son, and the tug of the Spirit.

Jen and I are taking some big steps of faith in our neck of the woods. Shortly after what we both found to be troubling election results, Jen was in England for a conference for church planters. She was distraught, tears arriving without invitation. After one session, she wrote these words:

> Day 2 (final) of the conference was remarkable! The church is in the center of Birmingham, built in 1100, freezing, but the singing...! We have done traditional church choruses, and after a fitful night's sleep and the desperate need to discuss shitty Trump with a woman, God delivered, hand to heart, Paula, a miracle. The keynote speaker was Debra Green, who started Redeeming Our Communities while pregnant with her third child, birthed the movement the day the baby was born. She sat across from me (you know that church shape, the cross, stage in the middle) and watched me. I wept, wept, wept, through 'In Christ Alone', particularly the part about no life in death and resurrection and all that, didn't help that an Englishman with a lovely tenor popped in behind me. I wept and recovered barely. She gave her talk, about how God woke her up in the night with a fire in her belly, a mother of three, etc. So much my story.
>
> Afterwards she grabbed my hand and said in the best English, 'God's got a word for you. I almost called you out in my main session but it wasn't appropriate. I thought of your scarf. I

was looking at it and realized my word won't require you to buy a new scarf or even to take it off. You just need to make a slight adjustment.' I swear, Paula, I told her nothing of our work, no specifics. I cried and she cried and she prayed with me right there. We talked Trump and she said, 'I know you are going to do something massive in the US, just looking at you, I know it.'

So, if we are being prayed over by her we are going to do incredible things! I have the utmost confidence God spoke to me today through her. There is no other explanation. She God-mothered me and now I get to come home and do this work.

We are grieving and we need to grieve. It comes in waves and the men don't seem to need to – only the women and minorities. So, we will. We will grieve well, we will grieve complete, we will grieve because something fundamental to who we are as a people, a nation, has died.

We can discuss the rising later; it's too soon. This is the middle Saturday. And you are amazing and fabulous and going to rise to partner with this world – when it's time.

Take care of yourself! I love you.

When I read Jen's email in my thin-walled hotel room, I was in New Jersey, speaking for a conference for parents of transgender children. As I began reading I buried my face in a hand towel and sobbed. An hour later I rose up and the towel looked like the Shroud of Turin, mascara and makeup outlining a transformed human face.

Two nights later I was back in Denver. Awakened by a dream at 4.00 a.m. I stared at the window, restless. I had dreamed I was at a party in which there was no food. A certain president-elect promised to find food and drove us to a fast food restaurant. When he discovered he did not have a credit card, I paid for the food. Upon returning to the house there was a woman in the living room who had not been there previously. The woman was caring for an orphan. She greeted me and said, 'You are safe. I am here for you, because there is much work to do. You will be all right. I am certain.' The woman had a unique look, unlike anyone I had ever seen before. Awake and staring out the window, I tried to place the woman. Suddenly I leapt out of bed and turned on my laptop. I searched the internet for 'Debra Green' and there she was, the woman in my dream!

Paul would have attempted a logical explanation for the visitation from Debra Green. Coincidence maybe, or possibly I had seen a picture of her in the past. Paul would have been desperate to find a rational reason for having a vivid dream about a woman I had never seen before. Paula had no such need. Call it what you will – synchronicity, the collective unconscious – I really don't care. I believe Debra Green was in my dream because the Ultimate Lover placed her there.

My life is not easy. My loving family still must struggle with my transition. I cannot find good work that pays. Most of my old friends are gone, never to return. But I am loved by the Lord of the Universe, just as I am, and I am discovering that is enough.

If I could go back and speak to that four-year-old girl in a boy's body, I would give her this message: 'This is the secret you must know. You, my precious dear, are loved by your Creator, just as you are. Now go, little girl, and live the life you were meant to live.'

Unwanted Gifts

The Revd Canon Peter Leonard

Reverend Peter Leonard started working in marketing and PR and was ordained into the Church of England in 1997, serving four years as a curate and then seven years as a parish priest in the Guildford Diocese. He then felt called into education and became a primary school teacher for seven years ending up as head of a school in Waterlooville. He now works as Canon Chancellor of Portsmouth Cathedral on the south coast of the UK, responsible for the education and community engagement of the Cathedral. Peter is a Trustee of OneBodyOneFaith, a group working for equality of LGBT+ people in the Church. He lives with his partner Mark and their two grown-up children.

'Can I ask you a question?' asked the eager Year 8 pupil at the beginning of a spirituality day in Portsmouth Cathedral. We often hold events for children and young people at the Cathedral, and on this day, we were looking at being whole people – body, mind, and spirit – through a range of interactive workshops.

'Of course you can!' I replied.

'If we are all God's children, why are gay people excluded from the Church?' Children and young people have the incredible ability to get straight to the point without any dithering. It did, however, take me by surprise as I saw in the face of that young boy evidence of the

143

damage caused by the Church's official negative stance towards LGBT+ people.

I answered him by saying that the majority of Christians did not exclude gay people and that many, many churches, like Portsmouth Cathedral, fully included them. I told his teacher that as an openly gay priest I was happy to come into the school and talk to the children.

I remember having my first sense of being different, of being gay, when I was at school. So, I'm always keen to be a positive role model, something I never had and which kept me firmly in the closet.

When I did finally come to terms with being gay, the song I listened to over and over again on repeat was 'Gethsemane' from *Jesus Christ Superstar* by Andrew Lloyd Webber (show tunes – see, the clues were there!). But it wasn't so much the music as the meaning I saw in the lyrics. It's based on the passage in the Bible which can be found in Matthew, Mark and Luke's gospels. Jesus has shared his last meal with his friends and is now praying, ahead of being arrested:

> Jesus came out and went, as was his custom, to the Mount of Olives; and the disciples followed him. When he reached the place, he said to them, 'Pray that you may not come into the time of trial.' Then he withdrew from them about a stone's throw, knelt down, and prayed, 'Father, if you are willing, remove this cup from me; yet, not my will but yours be done.' Then an angel from heaven appeared to him and gave him strength. In his anguish he prayed more earnestly, and his sweat became like great drops of blood falling down on the ground. (Luke 22:39–44)

As long as I can remember, this passage has been one of the most important to me. It portrays Jesus at his most human, at his most honest, and in pain. My experience of coming to terms with being gay and of being a priest has been about this same honesty and pain.

I didn't start coming out as gay until I was twenty-nine, by which time I was married, had two children, and was an ordained Anglican priest. It was not the ideal scenario to come to terms with myself and who I am. The vast majority of friends and family were hugely supportive, some even saying that I was very brave for coming out. I felt embarrassed by this as I didn't even make a conscious decision to come out. I just couldn't cope with being dishonest anymore.

It was when I moved to my first parish as a newly ordained curate that I met a fantastic gay couple. This was the first time I had knowingly built a friendship with a gay couple and it was transformational to see them living the kind of life I knew deep down I wanted for myself. I was still pretending to be straight at this point. I had tried for many years for this 'cup to be taken away from me' and went to all sorts of lengths to change the way I was. Of course, nothing worked, and I learned to hate who I was and indeed everything about myself.

One day one of the guys in this gay relationship asked me what it was like being a priest. Without any hesitation, which is surprising as I had not been asked the question before, I said it was like being given an unwanted gift. It was wonderful and precious and special but life would actually be a lot easier without it. After a short pause he simply said, 'A bit like being gay then.'

I felt like I had taken a punch to the gut – that was exactly what being a priest was like and yes that was exactly what being gay was like, and I knew both very well. I had multiple unwanted gifts – I had opened one, when was I going to open the other?

In the Garden of Gethsemane, Jesus was given an unwanted gift and a path to take which while being transformational would also make his life much harder, would in fact take his life from him. In that garden, we see a man who has been on a mission, a mission which has consumed his life and that of his family too, and it is reaching a climax. We are almost at the point of no return, and yet there is still the possibility here of backing out, of running away and living perhaps an easier life, the life Jesus had maybe dreamed of. And Jesus knows it.

He prays – no, he begs – not to have to go through with it. The passage dramatically and movingly says that as he prayed his sweat became like great drops of blood falling onto the ground. That is some serious prayer. I suspect that anyone who has struggled with both their faith and their sexuality knows something of that type of prayer. 'Take this cup away, don't make me drink it, find another way.' Jesus holds nothing back. He is completely honest with God. This honest Jesus is one I can follow. I can follow this Jesus because he knows what it is to struggle, to not want to do or accept something but know it is the right path to take. To try to get out of it but to realise it must be done. To receive and open the unwanted gift.

And so I try to be honest. I'm a priest in the Church of England, and I happen to be gay. I make no secret of it but nor do I feel the need to tell everyone that fact as soon as I meet them. I live my life and sometimes that is great and sometimes it is hard but it is as honest as I can make it.

For Jesus being honest made a difference, he came out of the garden with a resolve to do what it was God wanted him to do. A quiet resolve which coped with being betrayed by a kiss, having to heal the very people handling him so roughly and coping with the shadow of death now hanging over him. Being honest has made me a better priest. After coming out publicly my pastoral work doubled over night. Was this because people trust someone who is honest? Or is it that they are happy to share their troubles with someone who has experienced troubles themselves? Either way being honest made a huge difference to me and my ministry as a priest.

I don't have to face anything like Jesus did, but I try to be honest. Honest with God, with myself, and with others about who I am and what I am trying to be, honest about when I fail and how difficult life can be. Even after coming out I spent a long time accepting I was gay but not really liking it, almost apologising for it. I would argue with those who told me it was a lifestyle choice, saying that it couldn't be a choice because no one would choose it. Why would you choose it when it made life so much harder? But over the years, as I have learned to like myself rather than hate myself, as my relationship with and love for God has grown and deepened, I've come to realise something – something very important. Being gay, just like being called to be a priest, is a gift. Sure, it might present challenges, but it is a gift.

I now work as Canon Chancellor in Portsmouth Cathedral, and I am totally open about myself and my partner Mark of ten years. My two wonderful children, my family and friends, the Cathedral community are all fine with it. So the argument about not choosing it because it makes life difficult no longer holds water for me. Life is pretty good and maybe the 'unwanted' nature of the gift has changed. Maybe my honesty with who I am, my honesty with God, and with those around me has changed things.

Being a priest is a calling not a choice and it is hard work, but it is also wonderful and so I would choose it anyway. After a long and painful, but honest, journey I can now say that being gay is also not a choice. But if it were, then I would choose it anyway. In the Garden of Gethsemane, Jesus went from being a victim to being honest and it freed him to follow God's will for his life. I refuse to be a victim anymore. By saying that being gay isn't a choice but if it was I would choose it anyway, I am being honest, I am refusing to be a victim, and this frees me to follow God's will for my life.

Gifts, unwanted or wanted, come in all sorts of shapes and sizes. They might not be about vocation or issues around our sexuality, but these gifts are always amazing. It might be time to unwrap them and begin to enjoy them honestly.

A Walk by the Lake

Danny Fluker

Danny Fluker is a Yogi, Blogger and an IT Professional, native to Atlanta. Danny is passionate about social advocacy and using social media to promote Black Boy Joy and narratives of inspiration, growth and collective inclusion.

We walked along a wooded path that ran parallel to her favourite lake. This was where she came to meditate and to simply get away a bit from the demands of life as a nurse.

We'd just arrived and were taking in the scenery of the longleaf pine and the cloudless bright Carolina blue sky.

'Do you wanna sit for a bit?' she asked. There was something on her heart and she had brought me here to talk.

'No, no, you are a walker, let's keep walking,' she said, immediately answering her own question.

So we kept walking.

We were in a serious courtship. The kind of courtship with engagement in view.

Things were going well – or so I thought.

On that walk, she proceeded to tell me that I had done nothing wrong but she had this unspoken, deep-seated, unsettling fear. She didn't know what it was or where it came from, but she believed it to be a sign from God – she couldn't go forward with the relationship.

I tried to rationalise away her fear.

I tried to convince her that fear doesn't come from God. She was undeterred.

She didn't want to revisit this same fear six months from now, further progressed into a committed relationship.

It was best to end now on this path in the woods along the lake.

I was heartbroken.

I began to cry, the sort of cry where a single drop comes down your face, but I was successful in holding in the rest.

In hindsight, I'm grateful the relationship ended and that my girlfriend trusted her gut. She had no idea I was gay and, as far as I was concerned, that wasn't a reality for me either. That was something deeply suppressed, denied, and certainly not named.

I was a man.

I was doing all the things a man was supposed to do.

I had a good job, I'd just bought my first place, and was pursuing marriage with a woman. That's what men do. Especially good Christian men.

After the break-up I threw myself into work to try to ignore my pain. I even moved to another city hoping that would help.

None of it did.

When I did come to terms with my gayness (something I had been deeply aware of since childhood but had never fully faced head on) a few years after this, it was through a book I'd read by a prominent author who advocated a life of celibacy for people like me. That book was a lifesaver because it was the first time I'd read about other gay people of faith.

Celibacy was the answer.

I joined an online support group of other celibate gay Christians. That was my world for the next three years. I was also part of a local Church.

I wasn't out publicly, but my pastoral leadership and close friends knew about my 'struggle with same-sex attraction'. They loved and shepherded me well, and stood by me in my efforts to not act out on my internal reality.

About a month after the US Supreme Court decision to legalise same-sex marriage, the pastors of my Church approached me and asked if I'd be willing to speak in a video that would be part of their sermon series on human sexuality.

In the video, I'd talk about how my commitment to celibacy as a 'same-sex attracted' person reflected my love for Jesus, and how according to Scripture this was the proper response for all LGBT+ people.

I was eager and willing to do the video. This would be my way of both coming out publicly and also sharing what I felt would be a helpful testimony to others.

I gratefully agreed.

The video never happened, though.

Months later, before filming, there were a number of changes happening in my life. First, I lost my dream job; shortly after, I sunk into this deep funk. Following that, I began to doubt whether or not what I was going to say in that video about how celibacy was the only way for all LGBT+ Christians to live pleasing to God, was true.

I realised that I knew nothing of affirming theology, nor did I have any affirming friendships with which to challenge my own deeply held convictions.

I threw myself into study. I read book after book, both non-affirming and affirming. I also met my first gay married couple on a trip to New York while visiting family. Affirming friendships followed as I became plugged in with local affirming gay Christians.

Slowly the posture of both my convictions and my heart began to shift. I realised that I was beginning to become compassionate towards affirming Christians, and I eventually extended that compassion towards myself.

The shift in my consciousness went from a place of viewing my queerness as dirty, broken, sinful, and alienating from God, to something whole, innate, good, beautiful, and able to be embraced and lived out. Although I never did that video, I did come out through my blog. In a sort of cathartic release, I recounted the story of my job loss earlier on in the year and how that sent me down a path of deep study and self-reflection on the faith and sexuality question.

I made a decision to stay at my Church even though they were non-affirming. I knew I was loved well there and I also wanted to show that affirming Christians were no less Christian and could bear fruit, serve, and do all the good things good Christians were supposed to do. This lasted for about four months after I came out until I eventually had an emotional breakdown.

I realised that the part of me that I saw as wonderfully and fearfully made, a gift and an intentionality from God, was seen by those who loved me in my Church as something sinful and to be denied.

I couldn't bear the weight of that perception and it crushed me in an emotional flood.

I left my Church after that emotional breakdown.

I spent the next several months away from faith communities. Not for lack of affirming churches to choose from (I live in a pretty populated city), but mainly because of the emotional toll I knew investing in an entirely new group of people would take. I needed a break.

Presently, I've been out and affirming for just under a year. It's been a difficult year.

I've tried to navigate both a second adolescence and the dating world, and I'm also trying to find a new faith community. Despite the difficulty, there's nothing more rewarding than loving all of me because God loves all of me. Being authentically and wholly myself has been an unspeakably great gift of life.

Spiritual Gift Receipt, Please

Ryan McMillan

Ryan McMillan lives in the thriving metropolis of Belfast, having recently moved from his family farm in rural Northern Ireland where he spent many happy summers 'digging spuds' with his three siblings. From potatoes to protons, he is now completing a PhD in theoretical physics at Queen's University Belfast where tea breaks prove to be more common than breakthroughs. Ryan was brought up within the Methodist tradition and has recently helped to set up an LGBT+ Christian fellowship group in Belfast to meet the spiritual needs of those on the fringes of the Church. He desires to see more inclusiveness and understanding of LGBT+ people across the churches of Northern Ireland, which is the only part of the UK where same-sex marriage is still illegal. In his spare time Ryan likes drinking fancy tea and playing the piano.

I'm twenty-five years old and have been a committed Christian for more than ten years. I was brought up in the context of a small, Methodist Church in a tiny village in Northern Ireland. I have always felt loved, welcomed, and appreciated at my Church. I have enjoyed a happy childhood and could not have wished for a more loving and supportive family in every way. However, there has always been a dark cloud hovering over me from which I felt I could never escape. Something I have been ashamed of and prayed about over and over again, wishing that it could be taken away from me. The thorn in my side.

From a very young age, I have always known that I was gay – even at primary school I was aware that I had same-sex attractions. I have never been attracted to girls, ever. I have always seen this as a 'problem'. I was not normal. Somewhere along the line, something had gone wrong. Until the age of seventeen, I had never mentioned this to anyone. I was certain that being gay was not something God wanted and I was determined to live a life that was faithful to His Word.

'Homosexuality is an abomination.'

'Love the sinner – hate the sin.'

'Homosexual practice is against God's Word.'

'Wouldn't it be awful if you found out that your son was gay? I just don't know what I would do.'

'If I found out we were getting a gay minister, I would be straight down the road to the Presbyterian church!'

These are just some of the comments I would hear at Bible studies, in conversations, and sometimes from the pulpit at church. All uttered by well-meaning Christians who believed they were defending the Word of God, and who love me (and whom I love) dearly. I am in no way resentful of these people and I understand their point of view, but I wonder if the same things would have been said (and in the same way) if they knew the impact they were having on me, and on so many others like me. What would they do if they found out they were sitting beside a H-O-M-O-S-E-X-U-A-L? Would they run to the nearest temple for ritual cleaning or banish me from the church? Of course not. But the reality was that comments like these were damaging me emotionally and spiritually.

Living with any secret is difficult, but when the secret involves your sexuality – an intrinsic part of your being that plays such a large role in your emotional development and social status – the toll it takes on your mental wellbeing is magnified greatly. For most of my later teenage years I was deeply unhappy. Depression came in waves, and I remember for periods of weeks going to bed every night crying and pleading with God either to take this burden away from me (make me straight) or that I wouldn't wake up the next morning. I could never have taken my own life – I couldn't do it to my family, and I knew that it was not what God wanted – but the feelings of wanting my life to be over were immense and constant at times. Nobody knew about this, not even my family or closest friends. How could they have? I was so good at keeping my sexuality a secret – keeping my depression secret was, in fact, easy.

I felt that either God was punishing me or that He had a sick sense of humour. I knew that I was born gay and there was absolutely nothing I could do about it so I couldn't understand why He would do this to me. The main factor counting towards my depression was the fact that I had no hope and saw no future for my life (no matter how many times I read Jeremiah 29:11). As much as I hated the comments made by a lot of Christians about homosexuality, I agreed with them. I had read all the Bible verses relating directly to homosexuality, and the message was clear to me that I could not be a Christian and be in a relationship with another man. Either be celibate and live a life committed to Christ, or be in a relationship and leave Christianity behind. The message was clear. The problem is that the deepest longings of my heart have always been to be in a committed relationship with someone and perhaps even to have a family of my own one day. There was no middle ground and both prospects lead only to the possibility of a half-lived life.

I mentioned that I had never spoken of my sexuality until I was seventeen. By that stage my feelings of depression, anxiety, and despair had culminated in my reaching breaking point and I couldn't see how I could keep going on the way I had for so many years. One night after a church service, I was speaking to one of my closest friends who could tell there was something on my mind. After around 20 minutes of trying to put my feelings into words, I finally managed to convey to her that I was gay without actually saying 'I'm gay'. She was shocked, but the love and concern in her response were undeniable. She had no words, but at that point I didn't need any. I cannot begin to articulate the sense of freedom I experienced from just that one person knowing after struggling alone for so long.

Unfortunately, the next week that same friend informed me that she had been doing a lot of research and had come by a book explaining that gay people can be changed by prayer. I never read that book and we slowly grew apart in the years to follow and never spoke about 'the issue' again. Despite this, the pressure release of finally sharing my secret allowed me to regain some sense of normality that continued through my university years. However, the immense feelings of guilt and self-loathing always followed me, growing stronger with time.

At the age of twenty-four, I finally moved out of my parents' house to a flat in Belfast with my best friend. Hiding your emotions from a big family is rather simple. Playing the piano for hours on end would seem like practice. Shutting myself away to read my Bible would seem like being holy. Doing excessive amounts of homework would seem like conscientious study. How could anyone have suspected they were techniques for isolation and distraction? Living with only one other person, on the other hand, is a different story, and it was not long before my flatmate could see that something was up.

I had been missing days at work and never wanted to talk about myself, and if I did it was always negative. It was only a matter of time before she would start to ask questions, and to be honest I had a feeling she already knew I was gay. 'You know that I'm gay?' I was finally able to say the g-word. Rachel indeed did already know, and for the first time I talked openly about my struggles and about my high-school crushes and about how I like short guys with blond hair and blue eyes… The more I talked, the more natural things started to seem. Rachel is also a committed Christian, and as far as she was concerned God had no problem with me being gay. That was simply the way He made me. More than that, she thought it would be OK for me to go out with another man! What?! Surely she was just saying this to make me feel better? How could a Christian who reads the Bible come to that conclusion? No. I had resolved many years ago to live a celibate life and I was not going to be swayed by some sympathetic notion.

There are references in the Bible to 'the gift of celibacy' or 'the gift of singleness'. Jesus himself even touches on the subject in Matthew 19. In my mid teens, I had resigned myself to the fact that I had been given this 'gift'. I had wrestled with it, and I wished this gift had come with a receipt as I would much rather exchange it! Although this resignation helped me to cope to some extent with my feelings, I still had no hope and no joy in my life. As a Christian, this is deeply worrying and perplexing: hope and joy are the marks of a true Christian, and I couldn't help but feel like my faith wasn't real. My deep longings for a partnership and family remained, no matter how much

I prayed or how much I read. This theology, however, had so taken root in my heart that I was prepared to live the rest of my life in silent despair: I love God with all my heart, and as a Christian I have a duty to uphold His Word in every aspect of my life. It came as a shock, then, when I recently found my long-held beliefs being challenged by the Holy Spirit and my whole world view being turned upside down.

A few months after coming out to my flatmate, I attended a talk by Steve Chalke in Belfast on his article, 'A Matter of Integrity'. This was the first time I had heard a biblical exposition explaining that a same-sex relationship is not necessarily against God's plan for my life. I was stunned. I really cannot emphasise enough the transformation that took place in my life following that lecture. I began to read other books and I kept hearing the same message that same-sex relations are not against the Bible. After some months, the message finally sank in, and after almost 20 years of struggle I had reconciled my sexuality with my faith and with God. For the first time ever I saw hope in my life. My dreams and longings of uniting with a man in a loving, faithful relationship could now be a reality. I can't stress enough the importance of this paradigm shift. I began to feel emotions I never knew existed. When I smiled, I meant it – smiling no longer with just my face, but with my soul. When I sang the words 'How deep the Father's love for us' or 'You're a good, good Father', I actually meant them. God really does love me after all – He didn't make a mistake when He created me. I'm no longer faced with the prospect of a half-lived life, but with the hope of an abundant life that Jesus promises to everyone who believes in Him.

Portraying the gift of celibacy as the only 'answer' to homosexuality is wrong, and the Church must seriously reconsider its position. Celibacy is indeed a gift to some people (equally for gay and straight people), but I believe to make the statement that all gay people have been given this gift is not only illogical, but unbiblical. The gifts of God are rich and diverse. To make a statement that all Christians are given the gift of prophecy, or of healing, or of leadership, based purely on their sexuality, would seem strangely prescriptive and not in line with biblical teachings on spiritual gifts. Moreover, when Jesus talks about singleness in Matthew 19, it comes with a clause in verse 11: 'Not everyone can accept this word, but only those to whom it has been given.' When someone is given a gift from God, it is clearly recognisable if not by themselves then by others, and it can be used to bless others and further God's Kingdom on earth. In this respect, I can say with confidence that the gift of celibacy has not been given to every gay Christian (and certainly not to me).

It would be naïve to say that I'm now complete and fully healed. Twenty years of depression, anxiety, self-loathing, constant hiding, and spiritual drought leaves its marks. I hesitate to say that some of the wounds may never fully heal and though I now have hope for the future, and have found a new dimension of faith, I am faced with an entirely new set of problems. As a leader in my youth fellowship, during a night of testimonies I felt compelled to share with the young people my struggles with depression and my sexuality. I knew that when I was that age, just hearing that another Christian was gay would have changed my life drastically and I wanted to afford that opportunity to anyone who may have been struggling with the same issues. It didn't take long before word got back to my minister and various council meetings were held to discuss what to do with 'the problem'. There was no concern about my faith – the root issue lay in my new beliefs that same-sex relationships can be blessed by God. Even if I wasn't publicly preaching these views, as it stands they are not in line with current church doctrine.

Though the members of my Church have on the whole been incredibly supportive of me, both emotionally and theologically, I have recently had to step down from my roles as musical director, youth fellowship leader, and church council member after ten years of service. This was not forced upon me, but it was a voluntary (and, I feel, necessary) decision to avoid a rift and dispute in our small church that I love so much. On top of that heartache, I have experienced loyal members of our congregation walk out because of this issue without even speaking to me. I even face losing one of my best friends of 14 years due to a disagreement in theology. I do not mention these things to pass judgement or seek revenge on individuals. Conversely, whether they know it or not, my love for all the people who have hurt me has only grown. When my heart had been well and truly broken, I started to see people in a different way; I believe in a way similar to how Jesus sees them. Instead, I have said what I have said in order to break your heart, for I feel more hearts need to be broken over this issue in order to empathise with some of the pain that so many LGBT+ Christians and non-Christians live with every day of their lives, mostly in agonising silence.

One can argue back and forth with biblical interpretations, and we can read and read and read. For me, coming out to my friends and family has been one of the best decisions I've made. For the first time in my life I have felt true joy and am at peace with God and with my sexuality. For the first time I have acknowledged that a life of celibacy is not the only option for me, and that has given me a hope and freedom that I have never experienced before. I truly believe that the process of me coming to terms with this has been Spirit-led and in God's timing. I think that our Church has an amazing opportunity to reach out to a lot of hurting gay Christians with a message of healing and of hope. Not only that, I believe this message will open the floodgates to many LGBT+ people who might otherwise never have thought a relationship with Jesus was possible due simply to their sexual identity. I believe teaching that loving, faithful same-sex relationships are as valid in God's eyes as loving, faithful heterosexual relationships will be the catalyst for a revival in our Church across all nations.

> For I am convinced that neither death nor life, neither angels nor demons, neither the present nor the future, nor any powers, neither height nor depth, nor anything else in all creation, will be able to separate us from the love of God that is in Christ Jesus our Lord. (Romans 8:38–39)

SECTION 3: REVIVAL

As we saw in the account of Peter in the Book of Acts, the simple experience of the Spirit of God moving among a group of 'unclean' individuals was all that it took to change the Apostles' and elders' minds and forever change the theology of the Church. The Apostles could not deny the clear evidence of the Spirit's work when Cornelius and his entire household were overcome by the Holy Spirit and proclaimed their faith in Christ as Lord. What if, in our modern era, there was evidence of a similar move of the Spirit of God among a most unlikely people, who are confessing their faith in Christ? Would the Church be faithful to respond to the evidence of God's Spirit and move beyond a toxic, rigid theology to embrace greater inclusion and acceptance for sexual and gender minorities in the life of the Church?

A 2014 Gallup poll[1] found that nearly 53 per cent of LGBT+ people identified as 'moderately' to 'highly' religious, numbers that starkly contrast with the stereotypical image cast by many in modern culture who see LGBT+ people as non-religious. In 2015, the

---

1   Frank Newport, 'LGBT Population in U.S. Significantly Less Religious', Gallup. com (2014), www.gallup.com/poll/174788/lgbt-population-significantly-less-religious.aspx.

Pew Research Center released a report[2] that showed that nearly half (48 per cent) of all LGBT people in the US identified as 'Christian'. This number had increased from 42 per cent in 2013, and stood in stark contrast to the overall decline in Christianity among nearly every other demographic in the US. LGBT+ Christian activist Matthew Vines responded to the report's results in a piece by Eliel Cruz in *The Advocate* magazine, saying:

> The 'Christians vs. LGBT people' narrative that we hear so often is part of the story, but as the Pew poll shows, it's not all of it. In fact, it's the 48 percent of LGBT Americans who are Christians who are best positioned to change both religious attitudes about same-sex marriage and secular attitudes about religion. As LGBT Christians continue to find their voice, they'll be changing both their churches and the LGBT community for the better.[3]

Clearly, these numbers suggest that something dramatic is under way that could forever change the American religious landscape. While nearly every other demographic is declining in affiliation with Christianity, the LGBT+ demographic is slowly but consistently growing in their identification with the Christian faith. This is demonstrated, not just in abstract poll numbers, but also in events taking place across the country every year.

In 2016, the Gay Christian Network hosted its national conference in Pittsburgh, Pennsylvania, drawing more

2   Pew Research Center, 'America's Changing Religious Landscape', 12 May 2015.
3   Eliel Cruz, 'REPORT: Half of LGB Americans Identify as Christian', *The Advocate* (2015), www.advocate.com/politics/religion/2015/05/12/report-half-lgb-americans-identify-christian.

than 3000 LGBT+ Christians from around the world together to worship, hear biblical teachings, and network with other like-minded LGBT+ people.[4]

The number of attendees has consistently grown since the first conference took place in 2003. Similarly, the Reformation Project's conferences draw hundreds of LGBT+ people together multiple times a year for intense biblical education and inclusive Christian theology.[5] In Europe, the European Forum of LGBT Christian Groups represents thousands of LGBT+ Christians who are working to form Christian communities that include and embrace all people, regardless of their sexual orientation or gender identity. In 2003, the Episcopal Church appointed Revd Gene Robinson to be the first openly LGBT+ bishop in Episcopal history[6] and, in 2016, the United Methodist Church appointed Revd Karen Oliveto to be the first openly LGBT+ bishop in Methodist history.[7] In 2015, I became the national spokesperson of Evangelicals for Marriage Equality, the first national, pro-marriage equality, and Evangelical organisation in American history,[8] representing the views of nearly 50

4   Jonathan Merritt, '3 Christian Conferences, 3 Approaches to LGBT Issues', *Religion News Service* (2016), http://religionnews.com/2014/10/27/3-christian-conferences-3-approaches-lgbt-issues/.
5   Merritt, '3 Christian Conferences, 3 Approaches to LGBT Issues'.
6   Laurie Goodstein, 'Openly Gay Man is Made a Bishop', *The New York Times* (2003), www.nytimes.com/2003/11/03/us/openly-gay-man-is-made-a-bishop.html.
7   Jennifer Brown, 'Methodist court says first openly gay bishop is in violation of church law, should face trial', *The Denver Post* (2017), www.denverpost.com/2017/04/28/gay-bishop-karen-oliveto-methodist-church/.
8   Brandan Robertson, 'Evangelicals for Marriage Equality: The Story Behind Our Launch', *TIME* (2015), http://time.com/3308983/evangelicals-for-marriage-equality-the-story-behind-our-launch/.

per cent of millennial Evangelicals who enthusiastically supported same-sex marriage.[9]

These numbers and examples suggest that something momentous is taking place in the Church, and the fruit of this movement is good. More LGBT+ people are proclaiming their commitment to walk in the rhythms modelled by Jesus Christ. More LGBT+ leaders are rising up with inspiring visions of faithfulness, justice, and hope for the future of Christianity. More lives are being saved by the message of the unconditional love of God found in the Gospel. All of this evidence seems to suggest that what is taking place is truly a move of the Holy Spirit, and thus is a call to the Church to move beyond its static doctrines and rigid interpretations of Scripture to embrace the new thing that God is doing in our day among sexual and gender minorities.

In the Book of Acts chapter 5, the Apostles are arrested and put into prison by the High Priest for proclaiming the Gospel of Jesus in the temple. As the Apostles were brought before the High Priest and the Council to defend their actions, their words only 'enraged' the Council even more, to the point that the Chief Priest called for their death. Just at this moment, Gamaliel, a respected Jewish leader, stood up and said to the Council:

> In the present case, I tell you, keep away from these men and let them alone; because if this plan or this undertaking is of human origin, it will fail; but if it is of God, you will not be able

9   Daniel Cox and Robert Jones, *Generations at Odds: The Millennial Generation and the Future of Gay and Lesbian Rights* (Public Religion Research Institute, 2011), https://www.prri.org/research/generations-at-odds/.

to overthrow them – in that case you may even
be found fighting against God![10]

Gamaliel implored the rulers to cease their murderous pursuits against the Apostles, claiming that if their work was opposed to the work of God, it would fail, and at the same time, if the Apostles' work happened to be truly from God, the Council would find itself working in opposition to God.

As one considers the evidence – psychological, theological, and sociological – a clear and compelling case can be made that the Holy Spirit is, in fact, doing a special work through sexual and gender minorities in the world. Yet, at the same time, opposition to the work of sexual and gender minorities has continued to grow in severity in many of the world's largest Christian denominations, only furthering the harm that is done to LGBT+ people and preventing the swift expansion of the Kingdom of God. If the evidence suggests that the Holy Spirit is bringing about a revival and renewal through sexual and gender minorities, then the charge to the Christian Church universally must be the same as the charge issued by Gamaliel to the Council: if the work of LGBT+ inclusion is simply of 'human origin', it will fail. But if it is, as I argue, a work of the Spirit of God, then not only will opposition efforts fail, but they will also posture the Church against the very work of the God that we claim to serve.

Christians around the world are standing at a crossroads, and have a vitally important choice to make. Will we choose to cling to static interpretations of ancient biblical texts, rooted in a culture and system of knowledge that has been long outdated and improved upon, or will

10   Acts 5:38–9.

we heed the work of the Spirit of God who continues her mission to 'lead us into all of the truth',[11] calling us to explore higher ethical standards and calling us into biblical interpretations rooted in the perspective of the most vulnerable and marginalised in our midst? And though the Church has consistently failed to live up to its call to be a community for the marginalised, God's work continues nonetheless. As Cheryl Anderson writes:

> If the church fails to carry out the tasks of redemption and reconciliation, that failure does not limit God's actions… marginalization is a theological point of departure. As a result, our faith begins and ends in places of exclusion and struggle.[12]

The call of the Spirit is now and has always been to uplift and welcome those who have been seen as 'unclean' by religious groups and society. This is the example of Jesus, it is the trajectory of the ethics of the entirety of Scripture, and it is the call of the Church today. Until the heterosexual members of the Church are willing to sacrifice their privilege for the good of the LGBT+ community, they will continue to fail to walk in step with the Spirit of God and perpetuate a theology that brings death instead of the abundant life that the Gospel of Jesus promises to impart. But when Christians around the world recognise the good fruit being brought forth by LGBT+ people, along with the consistent draw of the Spirit towards greater inclusion, I believe we will get a profound glimpse at the world as God intends it to be, where every nation, tribe, tongue, gender, and sexual orientation stand as one in the glory of the Lord and the Spirit of Love.

11 John 16:13.
12 Anderson, *Ancient Laws and Contemporary Controversies*, p. 170.

Section 3: Revival

In the last section of the book, we will hear stories of great hope and progress. We will hear first-hand accounts of this revival that the Holy Spirit is bringing about among LGBT+ followers of Jesus, and be challenged to align our lives with the flow and trajectory of this new work that God is doing in our day.

The Journey Outside

Bill Drayton

Bill Drayton is sixty-nine years of age and has never been happier. He came out as gay in November 2011, helped by his then wife, with whom he still has a deep friendship. He used to try to please everyone, but only at the expense of his true identity. Having experienced bullying for most of his life because he was expending all his energy on maintaining his 'respectable' facade, he now by contrast is fully confident in his own skin, and therefore is able to stand up for himself without hesitation. After wandering through the darkness of self-imposed shame and guilt, encouraged in large part, implicitly, by those with whom he was in contact, he is on an exciting journey of discovery, which is marked by a sense of unconditional love, of which the source is without doubt divine.

We often want to put ourselves, others and even God into a box, in order to make sense of life and to feel comfortable, even if that comfort is based on a falsehood. Once that box is constructed, we don't need to think for ourselves, because it is dangerous. If we did, we might find we lose friends and even our families. Thinking requires 'stepping out of that box', metaphorically speaking, into unknown territory. We expose ourselves to unease, perhaps facing up to the possibility that all our preconceived ideas and beliefs are but dust – that, in fact, we have allowed ourselves to be duped into believing what the preacher told us.

That was my position, but God knows I was living a lie. Jesus said you will know the truth and the truth will set you free, because perfect love casts out fear. I was afraid to reveal who I really was, because I knew I would be condemned and lose friends. I hid my true identity for 50 years from the age of twelve.

I was a member of a charismatic, Evangelical Baptist Church for 16 years. I was used to the 'exercise' of the gifts of the Spirit, such as the speaking and interpretation of tongues, healing, and miracles. I now look back with a somewhat sceptical eye, seeing those times as being sometimes characterised by forms of brainwashing.

Up to the time of my release from 'prison', I suffered from depression and had two nervous breakdowns, which were caused by the hostile environment in which I had been brought up and was then living. A close relative had once said to me that if they had had their way they would have lined up queers against a wall and shot the lot of them. Clearly being gay was not an option for someone like myself.

Having come from an Anglican background, I became an Evangelical Christian and joined a Baptist Church. There were many times when I felt isolated from the congregation during services. The subliminal message which I was being given was that the secret about my true identity, of which I was ashamed, was absolutely forbidden territory according to the Bible. So, the dark cloud which hung over me became even more oppressive.

I tried hard to integrate into the fellowship, but it was always a facade. I could never let my mask slip for fear of 'being cast out into utter darkness'. I was always attempting to earn brownie points by doing God's work for him. I would seek to dominate conversations, not listening to whatever was being said to me, but rather being concerned about winning an argument – a sure sign of insecurity in my faith.

Nevertheless, I remember having a 'picture' which has become significant since I came out. For those unfamiliar with the concept of a 'picture', it is a bit like a daydream. The 'picture' was as follows: I was in a desert, wearing a heavy suit of armour. I felt constricted and hardly able to breathe. I was also parched. Then for some strange reason the armour just slipped off. At the time, I was disconcerted because I did not understand why I had this 'picture'. It made no sense.

I met a woman in August 1985, fell in love, and got married. She suspected from the outset that I was 'different' but because of her love for me, and knowing that if she challenged me I would have denied it to myself, she kept her own counsel. Looking back, I know that I married her to please my family, and for six months after the wedding I had terrible doubts as to whether I had done the right thing.

Our divorce was completed in July 2016 after 29 years of marriage. However, through it all, we have remained friends. We still have a deep affection for each other, knowing full well we cannot turn the clock back. In November 2011, my life completely changed. I had just come back from a trip to the US, and my wife picked me up from the station. It had been a long journey. At that time we were between houses – moving out of one and into another – and we were staying at a caravan park. She had read a book about a married man in his sixties coming out as gay, and realising this could be my story, she decided to ask me at a time when I would be at my most unguarded – jetlagged and exhausted.

After picking me up from the train station, she immediately asked me about my sexuality. For once I gave an honest answer, and it felt as though a great weight had been lifted off my shoulders. Remember the 'picture' I had had some while before I came out!

I believe it was because of her love for me that she made the decision to ask me, knowing that if as she suspected I were to answer in the affirmative, our relationship would never be the same again and that effectively our marriage would be over. She continued to show me amazing love when, despite the fact I left the home on three occasions to go to the Far East, she still welcomed me back – much against her family's advice. She was and is a truly remarkable lady.

As you can imagine, it has taken (and will probably continue to take) some time for me to be 'deprogrammed' from those aspects of Evangelical teaching which negatively impacted on the inner core of my being. The minister of the Church was not only charismatic in his theology but also charismatic in his character. He had been head of department at a secondary school and was definitely a 'man's man'. Whenever you went to see him, he would always sit behind his desk and you would feel like the naughty schoolboy, come to see the headmaster. He probably didn't mean to convey that impression but that was how it seemed, despite the irony of his being about 20 years younger than me. Most in the congregation looked up to him and would not dare to question his theology, because he was Bible college trained, and so who were we to 'rock the boat'? I wanted to make friends and 'join in'. If that meant fitting into a mould, then so be it. However, increasingly it was obvious that, try as I might, I simply did not fit in.

As it has turned out, my impression of many people who hold to Evangelical beliefs is that they have not critically reasoned out their faith for themselves and that, by just accepting things on face value without question, they are ill-prepared to engage with others who do not share their beliefs. I could have described myself in just those terms during my 'Evangelical' phase. I remember an occasion when there was a joint service for all the churches in our town. Afterwards I must have been waiting around the bookstall area, when a young lady approached me. Looking back, I realise she was probably a lesbian, and she was challenging me on my perceived acceptance of the standard view of homosexuality. My response was to verbally attack her, because I was terrified that my secret might otherwise be revealed.

I believe you can be so filled with guilt and shame about your attraction to members of the same sex as an Evangelical, 'Bible-believing' Christian, that you are in fact internalising homophobia. I was punishing myself for the unwanted feelings which ran counter to what I genuinely believed. I wanted to identify with a community which professed absolute and unswerving allegiance to a strict interpretation of biblical scholarship, but I always felt like an outsider looking in from a perspective of hidden but real doubts.

Coming out for me was the catalyst for a complete dismantling of this precarious edifice of faith. At first I believed that God no longer loved me because, as a gay man, I was now destined for hell. However, I then started from scratch, concentrating on the nature of a love which I had not previously encountered – either in church or elsewhere. This love was 100 per cent unconditional, as I allowed myself to discover.

I could not face dogmas or doctrines – particularly that of salvation. It presupposed our sinful nature, and of course this was a 'heaven-sent' opportunity for homophobic people to condemn members of the LGBT+ community as being not up to God's best, as it was put to me.

I have to say it has taken me a long time to disavow the validity of this view. I used to think that those who supported a positive interpretation of the Bible for gay people were trying to bend what the Bible says to suit their purposes. I wanted so much to believe in this, but doubts always seem to creep into my mind. Perhaps this was a throwback to my Evangelical times!

For me the healing has been ongoing over the last 18 months or so. In July 2014, I was out in the Philippines where I met my present partner. His maturity and spirituality go well beyond his years and have been a shining example of the outward display of God's unconditional love. He has a deep Catholic faith which has seen him through many a trial throughout his life, which has been characterised by a state of prayerfulness, and is not dependent on a regular, rigid discipline of church attendance. We both believe that God has brought us together.

I am now settled within myself, and at peace. No one can persuade me to go back into the shadows, pretending I am someone I was never meant to be. I know God does not make mistakes, and I am loved for who I am.

I returned to the UK at the beginning of November 2015 to complete my divorce. From April 2016, I have lived in Exeter in the south west of England. I have made a good number of supportive friends, but recently I made the wise decision to start going to Quaker meetings at the local meeting house. The meetings of the British Quakers are held in silence – which can have a very therapeutic effect on one's wellbeing. It is a collective stillness, which is punctuated by occasional short contributions to edify the meeting. All are literally welcome. There is no side to the Quakers. They see the divine in every person they encounter, and this knowledge colours all their relationships. I am not a Quaker yet. I am what is known as an attender. As a relative newcomer, I have just as much right to speak, if led to do so, as the oldest surviving member. So there are no hierarchies. I also value their commitment to good causes such as peace-building, reconciliation, and human rights. I very much like the name used for the Quakers – the Religious Society of Friends.

From the past, I can see that I have shed many of the negative aspects of my life which had dehumanised me and prevented me from standing up and being counted. I now look forward to living an authentic life, and to learning more of what it means to be human and in the light of God. The notion of God for me encompasses both my faith and doubt at the same time, both equally and comfortably co-existing.

I believe we all share a common, innate sense of the divine, which we can call God and which is frankly too amazing for us to understand but which nevertheless is a creative force of absolute, pure love – a personality fully involved in the universe, and shown in the person of Jesus in human form, thus linking us with the divine nature.

I am a Son of God

Andrew Deeb

Andrew (Andy) Deeb grew up in Ann Arbor, Michigan. He currently is a Master of Divinity student at San Francisco Theological Seminary. Andy graduated from Concordia University Ann Arbor in 2016 with a degree in pre-seminary studies/theological languages. Andy is the music minister at gathering-desire, a Disciples of Christ congregation in San Anselmo, California.

I identified as male from the time I could talk. It wasn't until elementary school that I fully realised I wouldn't wake up one morning with my body reflecting my identity. I didn't have a word for what I was until eighth grade. I tried to come out in tenth grade. My parents weren't supportive to say the least, so I dropped it.

In my senior year of high school, I realised I needed to transition in order to keep living. I had always known, but I didn't want to face it. I slowly started coming out when I was eighteen. I lost a number of close friends, some claiming that God hated people like me or that I was going down a dangerous path. I was ostracised and outed to those I wasn't ready to tell. Some people from my former youth group have since admitted that they were trying to get me to kill myself. They no longer saw me as human.

I publicly came out and began transitioning when I was twenty. Shortly before coming out I was walking to class and thinking about the possibility of transitioning. I went to a private Christian college and wasn't sure what the future held. I prayed, 'God, I can't do this unless you are with me.' Immediately I was overwhelmed by a sense of peace and the undeniable sense of the presence of God. Even though my attendance was infrequent in the months leading up to my coming out, I was concerned that my Church would not accept me. I talked to one of the pastors before publicly coming out, offering to leave the Church. He assured me that I was still welcome and my Church became a large part of my support system.

Likewise, much to my surprise, I wasn't kicked out of the college I was attending. They requested that I move off campus for the first year while they sorted out how to handle transgender housing. It wasn't ideal. I wasn't allowed to have a roommate and was very isolated. A representative from the student life office insisted on meeting with me every so often. I agreed and raised my concerns about my isolation and voiced a desire to move on campus. It was denied. Furthermore, I wasn't allowed to visit the dorm of either gender except for limited hours on certain days of the week. The representative also made comments about what bathroom I used and said something along the lines of 'it would be safer for everyone if you didn't use the bathrooms on campus'. I ended up filing a complaint with the Department of Education, prompting the school to request Title IX exemption[1]. The school then modified its policies to include language that excludes transgender people from

1 Title IX is a portion of the United States Education Amendments of 1972. It states (in part) that:

'No person in the United States shall, on the basis of sex, be excluded from participation in, be denied the benefits of, or be subjected to discrimination under any education program or activity receiving Federal financial assistance.'

campus facilities and gives the school the right to expel gender non-conforming students. All of this was done to reflect 'Christ-like values'.

During this process, I began to discern a call towards ministry. I began looking into the process of getting ordained with the denomination I grew up in, the Lutheran Church–Missouri Synod (LCMS). Initially they seemed okay with ordaining a trans person, as long as I remained celibate. Someone from an LCMS seminary said that my gender identity wouldn't be a problem, so I transferred to an LCMS college in order to prepare for seminary.

As I was finalising my transfer, I was informed that someone higher up in the denomination had decided that they couldn't ordain 'people like me'. Shortly after that, my Church decided that they didn't want to support my transition after all. The Church elders served me a letter stating that in order to remain an active part of the Church I had to agree to remain celibate, to not use the gendered bathroom in the church building, and to submit to 'special discipleship meetings' with the elders. They cited a number of Bible verses to support their objections. I tried to meet their demands at first, but decided I had enough after walking a half mile to a McDonald's to use a bathroom. I left the Church, and the pastor has since told the congregation that I am living in unrepentant sin.

A month or so after that I went in for bottom surgery. It went poorly. A few days after the initial surgery I was rushed back into the operating room with internal bleeding. Additionally, there was a malfunction with my morphine pump and I received a near fatal dose of morphine. As if that wasn't enough, I contracted an infection in the hospital that turned septic. It was during this time that I began to believe the things that my former

Church had said – that it was sinful to be the way I was, and God was punishing me for being transgender.

The year following was one of the darkest of my life. I believed God to be uncaring or angry and vengeful. Whatever the case, I wanted nothing to do with Him. I couldn't really run from God or the Church. I was still in college finishing up a degree in theology and biblical languages. My classwork forced me into the Bible every day and I eventually found my faith again.

I am now in seminary, majoring in biblical studies. Some of my current research interests include the portrayal of eunuchs in the Hebrew Bible, as well as the concepts of inner and outer person in the writings of Paul, and how they may apply to transgender individuals. My studies have led me to the conclusion that the Bible does not talk about transgender people. There are instances of gender non-conforming individuals in Scripture, but none of them can be properly equated to transgender individuals. The verses the conservative Church uses to exclude transgender people are being taken out of context and utilised in a manner that they were never intended. The rhetoric of non-affirming churches communicates that God created and declared all things good, except for LGBT+ individuals. Denying a transgender person the ability to transition is denying that person access to God. As Søren Kierkegaard says, 'the self connects with the power which created it in order to arrive at the true self. One must first know and embrace themselves before they are able to connect that self to any other force.'

My personal faith has recovered some, but I still have a lot of healing to do. Christian groups and establishments have treated me more like a problem than a person. I struggle to believe that I have a place in the Church. Despite this, I have found love and acceptance in Christ.

God was the first to confirm my identity as male by calling me His son. There is freedom for LGBT+ individuals in the Gospel. The Gospel of Christ is one of radical love and inclusion. The Gospel is unconcerned with drawing lines of who is in and who is out, but rather shows that we are all the same – we are all sinners made saints by the blood of Christ.

Who Owns God?

Christopher Arlen

Christopher Arlen is a minister, an advocate for gay men's health, and a powerful voice for spiritual liberation. He has developed successful programmes for the National Task Force on AIDS Prevention, the National Black Lesbian and Gay Leadership Forum, San Francisco's acclaimed Glide Memorial Church, and a host of others. He currently serves as membership chair at First Baptist Church of Denver. He lives in Lakewood with his husband, Damon, and their two dogs, Oliver and Sofia.

Here's the question: who owns God?

One of the great luxuries of time is the ability to stand in future age and look back and reflect on our collective past. When we look back today, it is easy to clearly see many of the great injustices that have been committed in the name in Christianity, the Church, or God himself. From our present vantage point, we see the Church's historical struggle with inclusion and acceptance – from the first century through to today.

If I were to share with you some of the great intellectual thoughts and writings of some of the religious and cultural thought-leaders of 1864, the vast majority of you would likely be stunned into silence by the ignorant and hate-laced words. Words penned by Christian men who held, in faith, faulty notions of white superiority and the so-called 'inferior races'. Hopefully, you, like me, would today consider these ideas to be unchristian, un-American, and woefully unholy.

For slaveholders, Christianity not only justified slavery, it was employed as a means of control used to religiously subdue their slaves. Slaves were taught to obey their masters with fear and trembling – as they would fear God. God, Himself, they believed, had decreed, established, and blessed the institution of slavery.

Many slaveholders viewed themselves to be good and upright Christian men. Some, even though they found themselves conflicted and afflicted with a moral unease about slavery, accepted that slavery was ordained by God.

One leading bishop of the day wrote:

> If it were a matter to be determined by personal sympathies, tastes, or feelings, I should be as ready as any man to condemn the institution of slavery, for all my prejudices of education, habit, and social position stand entirely opposed to it. But as a Christian, I am solemnly warned to be 'wise in my own conceit,' and not to 'lean on my own understanding'.[1]

Like many today, when it comes to LGBT+ issues within the Church, this bishop found himself torn between the rational humanity of conscience and the irrational orthodoxy of literalism. His personal dislike of slavery was in conflict with what he viewed as the plain sense of the Bible. The Biblicism of the pro-slavery movement

1   The Rt Revd John Henry Hopkins, Bishop of Vermont and Presiding Bishop of The Episcopal Church, writing in 1861 in *A Scriptural, Ecclesiastical, and Historical View of Slavery, from the Days of the Patriarch Abraham to the Nineteenth Century*, pp. 5–12 *passim*.

rendered rational judgement in the debate over moral issues a form of religious infidelity.

In fact, the Southern Baptist Convention, the second largest denomination in the US, and the denomination in which I was raised, was formed specifically to defend the cruel and unchristian institution of slavery. Looking back, it is clear to see – thankfully – that these attitudes, while seemingly justified by Scripture, were patently false and based in personal and social prejudices along with the religious ignorance of the age.

Likewise, Christianity was invoked against women in the 1900s to subjugate and control their place in society. And if I were to share some of the prevailing thoughts of the age about women, I'm sure you would likewise be appalled.

Think about it... at the beginning of the twentieth century, women were outsiders to the political system – unable to serve on juries, unable to vote, and deemed patently unqualified to hold elective office.

A woman had no legal identity of her own – she was simply an extension of her husband. His identity was hers. She had no rights when it came to consent or reproduction. She could hold no property of her own. She was unable to pursue the career of her choice. The Supreme Court even once ruled that women were not considered persons under the Fourteenth Amendment to the Constitution.

Many in the Church used the Bible to subdue and control women. As women struggled for their rights, arguments about nature and social order were used to undermine nearly every attempt to improve the standing of women. Scripture held, they falsely believed at the time, that a woman's place was in the home – taking care of her man and her family – certainly not as an engaged citizen.

Judge these words for yourself:

> The appropriate duties and influence of woman are stated in the New Testament… The power of woman is in her dependence, flowing from the consciousness of the weakness which God has given her for her protection… When she assumes the place and tone of man as a public reformer, she yields the power which God has given her – and her character becomes unnatural.[2]

Both the abolition of slavery, and the inclusion and empowerment of women in society were at one time considered to be atheistic pursuits. Abolitionists who were Christian were condemned as heretics or infidels. Those Christians who supported the women's suffrage movement were viewed as apostates – abandoning the love of God, and the fellowship of mainstream Christianity.

Even closer to the present age, one can view the landmark civil rights case *Loving v. Virginia*. Mildred and Richard Loving were a young interracial couple. They were not activists, nor were they seeking to lead or be part of a movement – they were simply a man and woman who fell in love and wanted to spend their lives together, as man and wife.

In the early half of this century, the Christian Church played an unfortunate role in stigmatising interracial marriage in the US. White supremacy and 'racial purity' were justified by stereotyping interracial unions

2   Excerpt from '*Pastoral Letter*', The General Association of Congregational Ministers, Brookfield, Massachusetts, June 27, 1837.

as sexually perverted and sinful – especially for 'good' white Christians. If a white Christian man were to look upon a black woman with interest – he was taught – the wrongness of his action would immediately seize him and convict him in his spirit.

In 1958, the Lovings found themselves awakened in the bedroom of their house by the police. They had violated the Virginia Racial Integrity Act of 1924, which forbade interracial marriage. Faced with prison, the Lovings were forced to leave the State of Virginia for a period of 25 years. When they could no longer tolerate being away from their families, their friends, their support systems, they returned to Virginia and were arrested.

The trial judge, with his own biases and convictions, invoked the religious ignorance and prejudices of the age when we wrote in his opinion:

> Almighty God created the races white, black, yellow, malay and red, and he placed them on separate continents. And but for the interference with this arrangement there would be no cause for such marriages. The fact that he separated the races shows that he did not intend for the races to mix.

Fortunately, this arcane and wrong-headed ruling was overturned by the Supreme Court in 1967.

When the Court heard *Loving v. Virginia*, the justices voted unanimously to strike down the Virginia law, with Chief Justice Warren writing that 'the freedom to marry has long been recognized as one of the vital personal rights essential to the orderly pursuit of happiness by free men'. This landmark ruling led to the overturning of miscegenation laws in 15 states. This precedent also factored into the Supreme Court of the United States' marriage equality ruling in June 2015.

So, from my perspective, looking through the long lens of time – racist, sexist, and bigoted attitudes born of Christianity have been the norm. I have been gay for as long as I have been black – the two are intertwined in my spirit, my heart, and my psyche.

This is my testimony and my witness: each of us bears the great privilege and responsibility for finding God for him or herself. Throughout history, there has existed the need for humankind to find new ways to know and experience God. In the Baptist tradition, we refer to this as 'soul liberty' – which is to say that we embrace a deep conviction that every person can enter into direct relationship with God without any outside mediation.

Standing at the intersection of race, sexuality, and faith, I can do nothing other than to trust the eternality of my spirit to God. I cannot accept what has been said about black people and race in the name of God and still love Jesus as my Saviour. I cannot subjugate and objectify women because God somehow planned for this as the 'natural order'. Nor can I absolutely not love my biracial nephews, my white brother-in-law, my white husband, or the many interracial couples who have cultivated loving relationships based on trust, integrity, and mutuality.

But God is faithful. In every age, it seems that God has sent pioneering way-showers to help restless societies understand and address the challenges of the age – bold outliers who stand in the gap to bridge social issues, religious practice, and individual freedom. Theologies of liberation become necessary to see and celebrate God's unfolding plan for us all. History teaches us that our understanding of those who are different must always be evolving.

Our shameful history and the attitudes that supported the sinful institution of slavery continued on through the civil rights movement and continue today, as evidenced by the necessity of the Black Lives Matter movement. Attitudes towards women and their role in society have also evolved, yet we still fight for a woman's right to exercise agency over her own body. Women still make less than men for the same work. And I can attest that interracial relationships still raise the occasional sideways glare. But we *have* moved forward.

In time, I am convinced that those who come after us will look back at our age and judge our current struggle for LGBT+ inclusion – to be able to worship openly and honestly as we live lives of wholeness and integrity. I am hopeful that they will judge us well as we are being called to be the pioneering witnesses of our day – standing at the gate, welcoming the prodigals as they make their long way home.

So, the question was this: who owns God? The answer is simple and true: God belongs to all of us.

Gay AND Christian

Alison Lintern-Gittens

Alison Lintern-Gittens is a 41-year-old, gay, Christian woman who enjoys scuba diving, karate, and days out. She believes it's OK to be gay and Christian, and that you don't have to choose between the two.

I was twelve when I lost my mother to cancer in the May of that year, and went into a children's home in the December, at age thirteen; my life was empty. I became friendly with the neighbours, who had a daughter who was a little younger than me. They were a Christian family and one day they asked the children's home if any of us would like to join a small children's Bible study group in their home, one evening a week. I accepted their offer, so, along with my sister, who is slightly younger than me, we attended the group. We learned about different parables and had to memorise a Bible verse every week to 'win' a book token. When we had enough tokens, we could choose what we wanted from their small library. One of the verses that stuck in my mind the most was John 3.16: 'For God so loved the World that he gave his only begotten son. That whosoever believeth in Him, shall not perish, but have eternal life.' This was when I first became a Christian, aged thirteen.

A few months later, my crushes on women started to develop into something more. I used to fantasise about what it would be like to kiss a woman, or get close to one. I tried to hide these thoughts as I didn't think it was right, being a Christian and going to church. What would they think if they knew? God didn't like gays, did he? When I went to church, I felt awkward, like I didn't belong there. I would see other women a little older than me and try to not look at them too much, in case they knew. I carried on going to the Bible group for about a year or so and occasionally went to church with their family. One day, the group stopped, but my crushes didn't.

I was around fourteen or fifteen when one of the ladies who looked after us in the children's home noticed that I'd been a little withdrawn and different recently. She was only twenty-one at the time, but how could I tell her that I fancied her? I wanted to talk about how I felt, about my crushes on women, but I couldn't tell the one person I felt at ease with that I was possibly bisexual. I told her I had a problem that only I could figure out, that nobody could help me. The look on her face changed to one of fear and deep concern. She kept asking me to tell her so, eventually, I wrote on a small piece of paper, 'I think I'm bisexual.'

I was asked to go into the office and talk about my feelings and how I knew. 'Because I fancy you,' I said to myself in my head. She asked if there was someone I liked or was I with someone, but I wasn't. It was then that I came to the realisation that I was definitely not straight but was I actually gay, as I hadn't even kissed a boy.

Fast forward to age twenty-one, and I had joined the Royal Air Force (RAF), my lifelong ambition. I was an out gay woman to family and friends, but not to the Service. Being gay in the military was forbidden during my first few years, until a law was finally passed that it was permissible. I had had a few girlfriends by this time, so my sexuality was steadfast. I hadn't gone to church since I'd left the children's home (at sixteen) as I always believed it was a sin to be gay. While I lived on the RAF base, I became friendly with the scripture reader who was based at my camp and used to visit my building regularly. We talked about many things, from her time in the RAF to Christianity. I told her I was a Christian but hadn't gone to church for a long time.

I started to attend church with her but I still felt awkward; being in a Christian setting felt all wrong to me. I was hiding who I really was. Going to church finally became alien to me, and I stopped going. I left the RAF in 2002, aged twenty-six, having served five years. I was out to everyone by this time, including colleagues in the military. I didn't go to church any more – being gay was more important to me as that was the path I had chosen and I didn't think it was possible to have that as well as Christianity.

The next eight years of my life weren't great. I'd suffered in an abusive relationship, and became homeless, having to stay with friends and friends of friends. I became settled in my own place again in 2010. My home, my rules, with nobody to answer to or worry if I was late home from work. I wanted to be single for the rest of my life – that way I couldn't get hurt by anyone again – even though at times I prayed to God why He was letting this happen to me. I was single for the next four years, I had a job, and I was starting to enjoy my life. So, I decided it was time to make some new friends, as I had cut ties with everyone but my family to start my life over.

I went on a dating website and created a profile, stating that I was looking for new friends and not a relationship. Obviously, there were a few messages from women who seemed interested but these dwindled after a few days, except for one woman. She was like-minded, sporty, had been single for seven years, and also wanted to make some new friends. After three weeks chatting online, we exchanged numbers and she asked me if I would like to meet for a coffee. I was nervous as I hadn't been on a date for a long time, but I said yes.

I was a confident, independent woman after being on my own for four years and I thought to myself, 'you can do this.' The day came and my nerves were all over the place. What do I wear? Casually dressed, we met, had lunch, went to a pub, and spent the day doing various activities. Our coffee turned into a ten-hour day together. I was hooked. We agreed to meet again, which I was glad of because I liked her, I really liked her. I surprised myself. A couple of weeks later, after staying over on a Saturday night, she asked me if I would like to go to church with her the next morning. I said yes, and that I was a Christian but hadn't gone to church for many years. I knew He was calling me back; I had kept seeing John 3:16 printed on the sides of different churches over the four years that I was single. He was watching me, calling, waiting, and that's what I believe led me to my wife. He had a plan for me all along, letting me find my life partner and bringing me back to the Church where He was waiting so patiently.

I went to church the next morning; the welcome was overwhelming and completely accepting of who I really was. I was introduced as her new partner and was surprised to find that nobody batted an eyelid. Was this really what Church was meant to be like? I went, every Sunday, feeling more and more at ease and realising that it wasn't wrong to be gay and Christian. Why did I need to choose and not have both in the first place? This was when John 3:16 struck me the most… that whosoever believeth in Him. It never needed to be one or the other

– God gave his son so that we could live, I understood that now. I was baptised and brought into membership of the Church a year or so later. I finally belonged somewhere that accepted me as a gay Christian.

Meeting this woman had opened my heart again to God and He welcomed me back with loving arms; I couldn't believe how blessed I was. When I was in my twenties I never imagined that I would be able to get married to another woman in a church… our Church. I am still fully involved with the Church and I also go to a group there called 'The Gathering', which is a safe space for the LGBT+ community and allies to explore the Christian faith. I'm a married, gay, Christian woman who has finally found my niche in life, realising it's OK to be gay and Christian and not have to hide away from Christianity.

Do Not Wait: A Benediction

Matthew David Morris

Matthew David Morris is a student of theology, an internationally renowned musician and performer, and a Grammy-nominated songwriter living in Portland, Oregon with his husband and their family. He ministers in a number of capacities within and among the churches of the Episcopal Diocese of Oregon, and he is engaged in local activism for people experiencing homelessness and marginalisation. He spent several years engaged in the contemporary Neopagan community, and his current theological work centres around a belief that the God of the Christian faith is a God of liberative love, whose love extends to all creation. Part storyteller, part songwriter, part critical philosopher and theologian, Matthew David's words aim to lay bare with poetic care the harder truths of our day. More of his writing can be found at matthewdavidmorris.com.

Do not wait until it makes sense to love me.
Love me now.
Love me fearlessly.
Love me in spite of your non-belief.
Do this, and you will know what it feels like
to be loved by the One who made and who
adores you.
Do this, and you will walk the path of

The One who showed us that death is not the
end of love.
Do this, and the Love which gave birth to all
being,
The Love which resides deep within your own
self,
will pour forth from your lips like rain,
nourishing the earth
and healing the wounds
inflicted upon us
all.
But do not wait.
Love me now.

We are each home to a small piece of the Holy. God's
love is fierce, and we are called to join God in that sacred
fierceness.

God will not be cast out. It simply cannot be done. Our
hearts are already occupied, as is this world. The holy fire
of God burns as brightly now as it ever has. Pentecost is
a perpetual flame that burns within the hearts of God's
children. The God who ignites this fire in you, inspiring
you to lift your arms in praise, is the same God that moves
me to dance, to sing along with Aretha and Whitney, to
transgress the cultural expectations that have been placed
upon us both.

God transgresses culture at every turn, Amen?

God is bigger than our institutions; bigger than our best
attempts at goodness.

And I welcome God into my heart. This God who was,
and is, and will be Love Incarnate is no more absent
from my heart than my heart is absent from my chest. I

welcome God in again and again, and I will do so as many times as it takes for it to be known that God was always already there.

I welcome God into my heart through my kindness and compassion. I welcome God into my heart by witnessing to the movement of God's Spirit through this world. I welcome God into my heart when I dance and celebrate the gift of this flesh, formed inside the body of a woman. I welcome God into my heart each time I proclaim that the Kingdom of God that Jesus so persistently described is in fact a *kin-dom*; one in which we are *all* God's beloved. This kin-dom is so thoroughly permeated with an awareness of God's presence and love that it becomes unthinkable to cast a person out; for to cast out one of God's creation is to cast out the Creator, and the Creator cannot be cast out.

So, neither should we cast out those whom the Creator claims as beloved.

A church that does not love and look to the witness of those living on the margins is a Church of Non-belief. Christians become non-believers the moment we assume that God is not already animating and illuminating the lives of the outcast. We become non-believers the instant we judge one of God's children as worthless. We become non-believers when we lock a person out of our communities for the sake of our own piety. As one who has seen the Church from both inside and out, I can testify to this. It can feel barren on the outside. Desert-like.

But God moves through the desert, too. There is no place where God is not present. God is moving in the club. God is speaking through the drag queen. God is changing lives in ways that Sunday Morning Christians don't even realise. God raises the dead as quickly as we execute them, because the love of God is stronger than any violence we can inflict upon one another.

God's love is paramount.

And this is the point I'm trying to make: none of us has a monopoly on God. We cannot claim God as our own at the exclusion of another person. It's simply not possible. God is infinitely more generous than we are. When we pull back, God moves forward. When we refrain, God indulges. We articulate our conditions; God offers eternal life. God cares nothing for our religious posturing. God, through Jesus, asks only two things of us:

Love one another, and love God.

Period.
End of story.
Done.
Finished.
That's. It.

Love God so much that you don't have to question whether or not to love me.
Love me so much that you don't have to wonder whether or not you love God.
Love with an abandon that can birth the universe.
Love with a generosity that can raise the dead.
Love with a relentlessness that can save the nations.
Love beyond your doubt, your fear, your anxiety, and your pain.

And in the moment that you think you should judge, love.
In the moment you lean toward unkindness, love.

In the moment when you listen back to that one sermon you heard, when the preacher sowed a seed of doubt in your mind about whether or not I was worthy of your love, suggesting to you that perhaps loving should feel more like suspicion, or unbelief, or distrust...

Love.

Do not listen to the voices that suggest that there is another viable option besides love.
Do not listen to the pundits that encourage anything other than love as a viable platform.
Do not proclaim anything other than love, because you and I are made of love, as was Jesus.

And if we are to follow in the footsteps of the Saviour, we better get used to the feeling of love in our bodies. We better get so practised in this love that when Jesus returns he will instantly recognise that the world that we have helped to cultivate is the same world that he described some 2000 years ago.

Love is happening. Right now.
Get on board. Do not wait.

Love me.
I am your neighbour.
God made me, just as God made you.
Love me for the sake of your own salvation.
Love me, because the end is coming, and it is already here, and there is no better moment to love than the present.

Let God into your heart.
Remember where you came from: love is the origin.
Love, sacrificed in a world hungry for power, is resurrected for the purpose of proclaiming the truth about itself:

Our Witness

Love was, and is, and continues to be.
Love God through me.
Love me, and in so doing, love God.

Love me in order that you might be more like Jesus.

Do it now.

Do not wait.

Love me, just as God loves you.

CONCLUSION

CONCLUSION

An Invitation

In these pages, you have read the stories of struggle, pain, faith, and love that make up the experience of so many LGBT+ Christians from every walk of life and background. You have read about the many ways that the Body of Christ has failed us and harmed us. You have read of our resilience and faithfulness even in the midst of the most severe persecution and oppression. You have read of our vision for the future, of a Church and a world where all are welcomed to step boldly into their place at the table of God's grace.

Now the question you must ask yourself is this: *what now will I do?*

Will you put this book on the shelf and go back to living life as you were before you spent time with these stories? Or will you take a step forward, moving towards the Holy Spirit's call to inclusion, liberation, and love? Whether you are an LGBT+ person, an ally, or a non-affirming Christian, it is my sincere hope that you have been challenged by these stories and the faithful witness of every life contained in these pages. I hope that you are provoked to take the next right move, whether towards coming out and embracing your God-created identity, or seeking to lift up the voices of LGBT+ people in your faith community, or repenting of the harm that has been done by the Church and taking tangible steps to change the way the Church teaches about LGBT+ people.

But whatever you do, you now have heard the voices and seen the lives of this great cloud of queer witnesses, and I hope that you will carry us with you in your heart and mind in the coming days. I hope that our stories bring about conviction and hope, restlessness and peace, sorrow that turns to joy. Because the Holy Spirit of God is doing a new thing in the Church and the world through the lives of LGBT+ individuals, and this movement cannot be stopped. It is my prayer that this book serves as an invitation to you to join with us in the amazing work that God is doing, and that you will join us as the Kingdom of God is manifest all the more powerfully on earth as in heaven through us.

This is our witness.

ACKNOWLEDGEMENTS

Editing a book like this is no small feat. I have been so humbled and honoured by the whole process. The courage, vulnerability, and hope shared in the over 100 essays submitted from every corner of the globe has reignited my passion and belief that God is really up to something in and through LGBT+ people of faith. To the team at DLT for believing in this project, thank you!

To the amazing team that helped me wade through the first rounds of edits on the essays in this book: Sheri Rosenthal, Jessica Honeycutt, Brody Levesque, Michael Wright, Rhiannon Hall, and Ruairidh MacRae, *thank you* so much for your help. This project could not have been the amazing collection of stories that it is if it wasn't for your skillful proofreading and suggestions. To Pastor Ray Shawn McKinnon who financially supported the process of editing this collection and whose spiritual vibrancy always inspires me – thank you!

To the LGBT+ pioneers who have served as friends, mentors, and guides to me along my own journey of reconciling my faith and sexuality: Bishop Gene Robinson, Bishop Karen Oliveto, Revd Jim Mitulski, Rich Tafel, Vicky Beeching, John McConnell, Jonathan Rauch, Sharon Groves, Paula Williams. Your encouragement and witness continues to be the fuel that keeps me doing this work. Thank you!

Our Witness

To the innumerable great cloud of LGBT+ witnesses who have gone before us, paving the way for the work of the Spirit in our day, may you be honoured by our stories and our gratitude for the path that you have paved to make our journey easier.

To all of the LGBT+ people whose lives have ended far too early as a result of the toxic teachings and practices on non-inclusion, may this book serve as a solemn remembrance of your lives and be one more step towards the complete abolition of toxic, anti-LGBT+ theology in the Church.

To all of the LGBT+ people of faith who are still standing in the closet, may these stories be a reminder that *you are not alone* and that you are wildly loved, just as you are.

To our expansive, diverse, and creative God, who calls us out of the shadows and into the light of our Truest Selves, may you be glorified and honoured by this work, and may you use these stories to spread the Good News of your liberation and inclusion far and wide for ages to come.